After the Ball

email
Inter

JUL 20

Fintan O'Toole is a columnist with *The Irish Times*. His books include *The Irish Times Book of the Century*; *Shakespeare is Hard but so is Life*; *A Traitor's Kiss: The Life of Richard Brinsley Sheridan*; and *The Lie of the Land*.

AFTER THE BALL
Fintan O'Toole

NEW
ISLAND

Copyright © 2003 Fintan O'Toole

AFTER THE BALL
First published 2003
by tasc at New Island
an imprint of New Island
2 Brookside
Dundrum Road
Dublin 14

www.newisland.ie

The author has asserted his moral rights.

ISBN 1 904301 38 X

British Library Cataloguing in Publication Data.
A CIP catalogue record for this book is available
from the British Library.

Typeset by New Island
Cover and layout design by Public Communications Centre
Printed in the UK by Cox and Wyman

10 9 8 7 6 5 4 3 2

After the ball is over,
After the break of morn –
After the dancers' leaving;
After the stars are gone;
Many a heart is aching,
If you could read them all;
Many the hopes that have vanished
After the ball.

– Charles K. Harris, 'After the Ball is Over'

CONTENTS

1

GLOBAL IRELAND

Irish people like to see Ireland as an exceptional place. Our suffering throughout history is unparalleled. Our monks saved civilisation in the Dark Ages. Our religiosity is incomparable. Our literary achievements are unique. Our struggle for freedom inspired the peoples of the world. Our sense of fun is unmatched. The complexity of our dilemmas is unsurpassed. The leap we have made from pre-modernity to post-modernity is faster and therefore stranger than that of any other society. And because Ireland occupies a place in the world grossly disproportionate to its population, this sense of our uniqueness is often reflected back on us from the outside.

All of this is, of course, an illusion. Many countries, even in Europe, have similar experiences of struggling to secure their independence against larger neighbours in the 20th century. Many cultures have been shaped by the same broadly nationalist cultural revivals of the 19th century. Take, for example, this description of what happened with the Gaelic language in the late 19th century:

> The native language had survived only in the remote rural areas (the native élites had been assimilated into the dominant linguistic culture) ... During the nineteenth century, linguists and ethnographers collected together and standardised these dialects in the form of a written language with a settled grammar and orthography. Ironically, even if the peasants could have read this "national language", most of them would have found it hard to understand, since it was usually either based on just one of the dominant dialects or was an artificial construction, a sort of peasant Esperanto, made up from all the different dialects. Nevertheless, this creation of a literary native language, and the publication of a national literature and history written in prose, helped to start the process of nation-building, and made it possible, in future decades, to educate the peasantry in this emergent national culture.[1]

In fact, this is not a description of the Gaelic Revival, but of the precisely similar and broadly contemporaneous movements in Latvia, Estonia and Lithuania.

Irish experiences of the struggle for independence, of ethnic and religious division, of social injustice and of the race to break the cycle of economic underdevelopment are not at all unique. Ireland may differ substantially from the small handful of countries that dominated the capitalist system as it emerged in the 19th century. Its particular mix of characteristics may not be found in the same combination anywhere else. But none of those characteristics is itself unique. Indeed even the illusion of being exceptional is common enough and most small societies share it.

What makes Ireland interesting is not that it is exceptional but, on the contrary, that it is, in the early 21st century, an extreme case of a phenomenon that touches every part of the world: globalisation. This complex process, in which economic liberalisation, speed of communication and cultural homogenisation are intertwined, affects everyone on earth. It creates losers and winners.

The losers, most obviously, are the 2.8 billion people in developing countries living on less than $2 a day and the 1.2 billion extremely poor people living on less than $1 a day. The ratio of the average income enjoyed by the world's richest 20 countries to that of the 20 poorest has doubled in the past 40 years, so that the rich countries earn 37 times more than the poor. For all the fabulous technological progress that has driven globalisation, more than 1 billion people in low- and middle-income countries still lack access to safe water, and 2 billion lack adequate sanitation, leaving them prey to avoidable diseases and premature death. Nearly 2 million hectares of land worldwide (23 per cent of all cropland, pasture, forest and woodland) have been degraded since the 1950s. Eight hundred and twenty million people do not receive enough food to lead healthy and productive lives, and about 160 million children are seriously underweight for their age.

Many countries – such as Senegal, Somalia, Angola, Venezuela, Nigeria, Haiti and Ghana – had a gross domestic product (GDP) per capita in 1999 that was lower than it was in 1960.[2]

But the big winner in the globalisation stakes is Ireland. The Republic of Ireland is the most globalised country on earth. It is at the leading edge of a process that touches every part of the planet. This makes it the great test case for the successes and failures of the free market ideology that is driving global development.

For the last three years, the Washington-based *Foreign Policy* magazine has compiled the A. T. Kearney/*Foreign Policy* Magazine Globalisation Index. In each of the last two years, Ireland has been the top-ranked country.

A. T. Kearney/*Foreign Policy* Magazine Globalisation Index 2003: top 20 rankings

1. Ireland	11. United States
2. Switzerland	12. France
3. Sweden	13. Norway
4. Singapore	14. Portugal
5. Netherlands	15. Czech Republic
6. Denmark	16. New Zealand
7. Canada	17. Germany
8. Austria	18. Malaysia
9. United Kingdom	19. Israel
10. Finland	20. Spain

The 2003 rankings are based on the data available

at the end of 2001. The index ranks 62 countries, representing 85 per cent of the world's population, and is based on economic integration, technology, political engagement and personal contact. Economic integration is assessed by combining data on trade, foreign direct investment, portfolio capital flows and income payments and receipts. Technological connectedness is gauged by counting Internet users, Internet hosts and secure servers. The political engagement criteria are the number of international organisations and UN Security Council missions in which each country participates and the number of foreign embassies that each country hosts. Personal contact is charted by looking at a country's international travel and tourism, international telephone traffic and cross-border transfers, including remittances.

This is a wide range of tests and the index does seem to capture, not just the flow of trade and investment, but also the way people live and the way a government behaves on the international stage. And it is worth remembering that 2001 was a bad year for international investment and travel. Economic integration slowed down because of the end of the long 1990s boom. World economic growth plummeted from 4 per cent in 2000 to 1.3 per cent in 2001. Trade levels declined by 1.5 per cent, and global foreign direct investment flows dropped more than 50 per cent from $1.49 trillion to $735 billion. International travel, already affected by the downturn, was catastrophically affected by the September 11th attacks on New York and Washington. For the first time since

1945, the annual flow of international travel and tourism actually declined.

Yet even in this context, Ireland remained the star performer of globalisation. In 2001, Ireland attracted $91 billion in portfolio capital inflows – $11 billion more than the previous year and nearly $30 billion more than the United Kingdom. Ireland also expanded its international trade volumes on the strength of robust exports of computer components, electronics and medical and pharmaceutical products, ranking just behind Singapore and Malaysia in total trade measured as a share of gross domestic product. While the volume of world trade in 2001 declined by 1.5 per cent, Irish foreign trade actually increased. Ireland also emerged as the world's most talkative nation, with more than 737 minutes of international telephone calls per person in 2001, a reflection in large measure of the number of multinational corporations who have their call centres located here.

It is not just that Ireland is unusually globalised. It is also that the process of making it so has been driven to a huge extent from the outside. Since 1993, 25 per cent of all new US investment in the EU has gone to Ireland, which has only 1 per cent of the EU's population. By 2002, 585 American businesses operated in the Republic of Ireland, employing 94,000 people and representing an investment of $23 billion in the Irish economy. Of the €93 billion worth of goods exported from Ireland in 2001, the chemical, pharmaceutical and computer sectors, in which US corporations are utterly dominant, accounted for almost 60 per cent.

All of this is especially remarkable because it happened so quickly. For much of the 20th century, the growth of output per capita in Ireland was the lowest among 23 European countries, with the single exception of the UK. Up to the late 1950s, the Irish economy was relatively closed, even by the standards of small European countries, exporting 30 per cent of GDP in 1960 compared with 46 per cent in Holland and 39 per cent in Belgium. It was caught in the contradiction of a protected home market on the one side and a shrinking population on the other, so that the aim of economic independence was essentially unachievable. Even if Irish companies could use the protection of high tariff barriers to shelter their growth, the market that they were hoping to serve was in steady decline. Their intended consumers were emigrating. This inescapable bind forced the abandonment of economic nationalism.

The opening up of the economy began in 1958 with the publication of the First Programme for Economic Expansion. The removal of tariff barriers and the introduction of generous incentives to foreign investors paid immediate dividends. The rate of growth more than doubled to 4 per cent. The population started to rise again as emigration abated and the marriage rate increased. International developments, from the introduction of television to the Second Vatican Council to the rise of feminism, began to open up what had been a relatively restrictive culture. International trade increased rapidly: in 1960, 25 per cent of national output was exported; by 1985 it was 63 per cent. More important, the "international" in international trade began to really mean something. Independent Ireland had remained an economic satellite of the UK, to which 75 per cent of Irish exports went in 1960. By 1984, that figure had fallen to just 34 per cent as European and American markets became steadily more important. And through all of this, Ireland ceased to be a rural society and an agricultural economy. From 1971 onwards, a majority of the population lived in towns and cities. In 1960, 37 per cent of all Irish jobs were in farming, fishing and forestry. By 1987, this had fallen to just 14 per cent.

In broad terms, then, the integration of Ireland into the global economy has been underway for over forty years. But the pace and scale of the process increased beyond recognition in the 1990s. The dramatic shift of gear is obvious in the balance of trade figures (see Table 1.1).

These figures are reflected in a range of striking improvements. Huge levels of public debt were transformed in the golden years of the late 1990s into embarrassingly large surpluses. Within a decade, the unemployment level went from 17.4 per cent in 1986 to 3.9 per cent by the fourth quarter of 2000. At the same time the ratio of external debt to GDP – the best measure of how solvent a state is – fell from 120 per cent to less than 50 per cent. In 2001 Ireland was exactly twice as rich, measured in real terms, as it was in 1990.

Table 1.1 Balance of trade

Year	Imports €m	Exports €m	Trade surplus €m
1990	15,832	18,204	2,372
1991	16,317	19,070	2,753
1992	16,754	21,260	4,506
1993	18,900	25,179	6,279
1994	21,945	28,891	6,946
1995	26,181	35,330	9,149
1996	28,480	38,609	10,129
1997	32,864	44,868	12,004
1998	39,715	57,322	17,607
1999	44,327	66,956	22,629
2000	55,909	83,889	27,980
2001	57,384	92,690	35,306
2002	55,303	93,723	38,421

Source: Central Statistics Office

The Irish boom was never quite as impressive as much of the analysis, based on comparisons between Irish GDP and that of other countries, seemed to suggest. Because of the size of foreign direct investment in Ireland, and the associated repatriation of profits to the home countries of transnational corporations, there is a significant difference between gross national product (GNP) and GDP in Ireland. No EU country and only one OECD country, New Zealand, approximates the magnitude of the Irish difference between GNP and GDP. The concentration of economic activity in multinational high-tech companies and the relatively high level of external debt means that GDP, the normal indicator of output, overstates both the level and growth of Irish incomes. The level of GNP, a more appropriate level of income, was over 12 per cent less than GDP in 1995, while its increase was about 2 percentage points less than the GDP in the five years ending 1995. In 2000, GNP was 16 per cent less than GDP.

Nevertheless, the boom was real. From 1993 to 2000, the average annual growth of GNP was 9.3 per cent. The level of employment increased in the same period at the highest rate in the OECD: from 1.15 million to 1.65 million. During the 1990s, indeed, the percentage increase in employment in Ireland was almost 2.7 times that of the next best performing European economy, the Netherlands, and 4 to 5 times that of Sweden, Norway, Denmark and Belgium. Employment in Ireland even grew at double the rate of the then-booming US. And people with jobs were undoubtedly better off. Between 1987 and 2001, the cumulative increase in real take-home pay for a single person on the average manufacturing wage was almost 60 per cent. Even though social welfare payments did not rise in line with wages, they did increase substantially in real terms. Consistent poverty fell from 14.4 per cent of the population in 1994 to 5.5 per cent in 2000. The population of the Republic, now 3.8 million, rose to its highest level since 1881.

All of this was happening, admittedly, in the best possible circumstances. Ireland was joining a party that was in full swing. The joint was jumping. Globally, the growth in economic output in just three years – from 1995 to 1998 – exceeded that during the entire 10,000-year period from the beginning of agriculture to the dawn of the 20th century. The growth of the global economy in 1997 alone far exceeded that during the entire 17th century. More generally, the period of Ireland's economic development since the 1950s is one in which world trade has grown from $380 billion in 1950 to $5.86 trillion in 1997.[3] American firms invested more capital overseas in the 1990s – in excess of $750 billion – than in the previous four decades combined. In spite of the rhetoric of globalisation, this surge in US foreign direct investment did not flow to the new and untapped markets of the developing nations. Roughly half of the global total went to Europe. The book value of US foreign direct investment in Europe, which stood at just $1.7 billion in 1950, totalled $612 billion in 1999. Meanwhile, Europe's investment stake in the US, which amounted to just $2.2 billion in 1950, reached $640 billion in 1999. Total trade (exports plus imports) between the two parts of the world topped $500 billion in 1999, as against less than $10 billion at the outset of the post-Cold War era. It would have been truly astonishing if Ireland, as an Anglophone member of the EU, had not received a slice of this vast cake. If Ireland couldn't get its act together and definitively join the developed world during this period, and especially in the 1990s, it was probably doomed to fail forever.

It should also be remembered that the spectacular growth of the 1990s was in part a reflection of the spectacular failures of previous decades. The speed with which the economy took off strongly suggested that it had a pent-up potential which had been held back by bad policies in the past. For all the tendency to blame failure on the legacy of history, the truth was that independent Ireland had frittered away the relatively decent economic position it had inherited.

In the early part of the century, Irish living standards were comparable to those of northern European economies such as Norway and Finland, with per capita income levels of about 50 per cent of the UK, but greater than countries such as Italy, Greece and Portugal and were converging toward levels in Britain and most of Western Europe. Following independence, Ireland's relative position began to slip.

Comparing Ireland's performance between 1913 and 1987 with that of other western European countries produces a miserable picture. Switzerland started out with 81 per cent of the UK's real product per head of population and ended up with 130 per cent. Finland started out with 42 per cent and ended up with 104 per cent. Austria started with 65 per cent and ended with 96 per cent. Norway started with 51 per cent and ended with 127 per cent. Ireland started with 53 per cent and ended at just 60 per cent. To put it another way, Ireland was just 8 percentage points below the typical western European level of per capita product in 1913 and 35 points below in 1987.[4]

Looking back as recently as 1989, the historian J. J. Lee gave a savage summary of this performance:

Ireland recorded the slowest growth of per capita income between 1910 and 1970 of any European country except the United Kingdom. Every country ranked above Ireland in the early 20th century pulled much further ahead. Every country below Ireland either overtook her, or significantly narrowed the gap. The result was that Ireland slid from being a reasonably representative western European economy, in terms of income per head, at the time of independence, to a position far below the western European average in 1970 ... No other European country, east or west, north or south, for which remotely reliable evidence exists, has recorded so slow a rate of growth of national income in the twentieth century.[5]

Even bearing in mind the extraordinary circumstances of the 1990s and the artificially retarded state of the Irish economy, however, Ireland seems nevertheless the best argument for free market globalisation. While much of the population aspires to the high levels of social services that are associated with an active, interventionist State, and while the Taoiseach Bertie Ahern describes himself as a socialist, the mandarins of free market ideology in the US regard Ireland as a good example of their right-wing model in action.

The most prominent US neo-conservative think-tank, The Heritage Foundation, compiles an Index of Economic Freedom in association with the *Wall Street Journal*. In the 2003 Index, Hong Kong, the long-time darling of the New Right, is ranked first. But Ireland, ranked fifth, is very high up the ladder. The UK, for example, is ninth, Sweden eleventh, Germany nineteenth, and North

Korea one hundred and fifty-sixth. The US itself comes one place behind Ireland in sixth. To a Washington neo-conservative, it seems, Ireland is more American than America.

The Irish example was also cited approvingly by economic conservatives in Canada. Fred McMahon of the Atlantic Institute for Market Studies described the Irish economic performance of the 1990s as "nothing short of miraculous" and argued that this success proves the redundancy of Keynesian social democratic ideas:

> Ireland has been one of the globe's uncontested economic stars since 1987, when a new fiscally responsible, tax-cutting government was elected to office, and a society-wide agreement was struck to hold down labour costs. Ireland may now be the world's brightest star ... Irish policy-makers regard tax cuts and wage moderation – explicitly designed to reduce costs in the Irish economy and to increase profits – as the corner-stones of recent Irish success. In direct contradiction to the old Keynesian assumptions, this was accomplished during a period, of sometimes intense government retrenchment. This was particularly true at the beginning of the period, when spending cuts actually seemed to spark new growth.[6]

Ireland, then, seems to prove the validity of right-wing, free market ideology. The shrinking of government, the cutting of taxes and the reduction of public expenditure created wealth, even in a country that had previously been an economic basket case. By embracing the global market and following the rules laid down by neo-conservatives, Ireland prospered. And even if the rich did best, everybody benefited. Wages rose, unemployment shrunk, emigration turned into immigration and we all had the best years of our lives.

If all of this were true, Ireland would indeed be a very forceful argument for right-wing ideology. Most of it, however, is nonsense. Whatever else the Irish economic model from the late 1980s onwards may have been, it was not free market. It was driven in large measure by precisely the kind of institutions that the Right despises: an interventionist government, public servants, the social democrats of the European Union and the trade union movement. Even in strictly economic terms, the role of left-wing movements such as feminism was crucial.

It is undoubtedly true that the Fianna Fáil Government of 1987 to 1989 cut public expenditure as a whole rather drastically. In 1986 the current budget deficit was 7.9 per cent of GDP while the public-sector borrowing requirement (PSBR) was 14.2 per cent of GDP. By 1990 the corresponding figures had dropped to 0.6 and 2.8, respectively. This was achieved very largely by taking the axe to social spending, earning the finance minister of the time, Ray McSharry, the well-deserved nickname of Mac the Knife. Public-sector recruitment was frozen. Hospital beds were closed. Basic social infrastructure, like primary-school buildings, was allowed to deteriorate.

The cuts, however, were not evenly spread. That Government, which we now know to have been headed by the most corrupt politician in the history of the State, Charles Haughey, made sure that the people best able to bear the burden of reducing a catastrophic national debt were in fact able to opt out of the pain. The weight fell to a disproportionate extent on the shoulders of the weak, the vulnerable, the sick and the poor. Health spending, for example, which had been 7.3 per cent of GNP in 1981, was cut to just 6 per cent by 1989. The consequences of this imbalance, which will be dealt with in subsequent chapters, were profound and disastrous.

One of the crudest of logical fallacies is the assumption that because A happened after B, it happened as a result of B. The sun may have risen after I had my porridge this morning, but it would be rather odd to conclude that the consumption of porridge causes the sun to rise. The same is true of the sequence of events that preceded the Irish boom of the 1990s. That the economy began to grow rapidly after the Government cut public spending and services is undoubtedly true. If there is any relationship of cause and effect between these two events, however, it is at best a tenuous one. The evidence that the State was taking action to bring spiralling public debt under control certainly contributed to the economic improvements by making investors more confident. The emergence of a public consensus on the need to control the debt certainly helped to generate a wider commitment to a co-ordinated economic strategy, with wage demands being moderated in return for the promise of a more prosperous nation in the near future. But the Irish boom had many other causes, and the way the debt crisis was handled had long-term costs and consequences that must be included in any realistic reckoning.

THE STATE

The biggest irony of Ireland's iconic status among the neo-conservative champions of small government and despisers of the interventionist state is that if there is an Irish economic model it is one that has the fingerprints of big government all over it. The frontline troops in the battle for foreign investment were public servants working for the Industrial Development Authority, many of them showing a degree of motivation and enterprise that would have done any swaggering entrepreneur proud. Civil servants and politicians played key roles in negotiating the national partnership agreements that created a stable environment for investment. The consistent public policy of funding third-level education to increase the throughput of graduates created the pool of skilled labour that attracted the transnational corporations. (In many ways, indeed, the boom could be characterised as a simple reversal of a transatlantic journey. In the 1980s, labour went to where the capital was: the Irish graduates emigrated to the US. In the 1990s, the capital went to where the labour was: the US transnational corporations set up in Ireland.) A model neo-conservative state would have done none of these things but simply slashed personal and corporate taxes and waited for the market to work its magic.

In which case, of course, the number of university places would have contracted and the few graduates that were emerging would have continued to emigrate.

MAC THE KNIFE AND DOCTOR DELORS

Ireland was very fortunate that, just when the Mac the Knife strategy was being put in place, the European Union, then under the guidance of an old-fashioned French socialist Jacques Delors, decided to double the level of its regional, social and structural funding to poorer regions within the EU, a category that included all of Ireland. The Commission allocated IR£8,640 million to Ireland for the years between 1987 and 1998, inclusive. During the decade 1989–1999, these structural funds alone accounted for about 2.6 per cent of Ireland's entire annual GNP. The scale of this assistance, motivated in large measure by old-fashioned left-of-centre principles that were then dominant in western Europe, can be appreciated from World Bank estimates that flows of aid from the rich world to middle-income developing countries represent about 1 per cent of the latter's GNP. Aid to countries such as China and India amounts to less than this. Even this under-estimates the scale of EU structural funding to Ireland, as the EU money was all in the form of direct grants, while much aid to developing countries comes in the form of loans.

Most of this money was used to compensate for the cutbacks in public capital spending and employment training programmes. While EU subsidies had formed a very small part of the public capital programme in Ireland (just 0.37 per cent) in 1975, they amounted to between 5 and 6 per cent in the 1987–1989 period. Essentially, much of the flesh that was cut out of the public capital programme by Mac's knife was sewn back in again by Doctor Delors. Spending the German and French taxpayers' money is, in principle, no different from spending the Irish taxpayers'. And though the overall amount of EU structural funding was a relatively small part of total State spending in Ireland, it played a crucial role in saving Ireland from the worst consequences of the cuts in spending on roads, sewerage and transport. Without it, the 1990s boom, which in any event placed an almost unsupportable burden on a creaking infrastructure, might not have been possible.

There is, though, a much more profound sense in which the Irish boom would have been impossible without the EU. For membership of the EU had one massive, overriding effect on Irish society. It didn't create the conflict between tradition and modernity that we have lived with for the last fifty years. But it meant that that conflict could only be resolved in favour of modernity. Before the EEC, as it then was, you could just about make a case for an isolated, protected, conservative Ireland. You could propose that the main goal of Irish people was to preserve intact a set of religious, cultural and social values they had allegedly inherited from their ancestors. At least in the way Irish people talked about themselves, this ideal had immense prestige. Even though it was contradicted in daily life all the time, it still had behind it the authority of religion, of the education system and of political rhetoric.

The EU destroyed those illusions. Looking back, it's clear that one of the things the EU accomplished in Ireland is that it bought off the conservative heartlands of rural Ireland. Between 1975 and 1998, the EU's FEOGA price guarantees and guidance programme transferred IR£14,000 million to Irish farmers. In this way, the EU offered modernity in a form that seemed at first to be purely material. It was modernity not as sex, secularism and confusion but as green pounds, mechanised milking parlours, beef and butter mountains and headage payments. It seemed to be about money, not about politics, society or culture.

It probably helped that in the initial period of EU membership rural Ireland gained while urban Ireland lost out. In the countryside, new bungalows were springing up like mushrooms moistened by the sweet mist of prosperity that seemed to descend on the fields. In the towns and cities, mass unemployment was laying down deep roots as traditional, uncompetitive and labour-intensive industries shut up shop.

Before it quite knew it, the conservative heartland had bought into a modernising project much more radical in its implications than anything it could have imagined. The road paved with ECUs was leading inexorably to a transnational political union and a globalised industrial economy. Yet the economic benefits of following it, and the economic costs of trying to go back, were so great that there was no real choice except continuing to put one foot in front of the other.

Things came to a crunch in 1992 with the referendum on the Maastricht Treaty, when anti-abortion activists appealed for a "no" vote. Faced with a choice between taking a stand on the most visceral moral issue – one which had led in the infamous abortion referendum of 1983 to what an *Irish Times* editorial called "the second partitioning of Ireland" – and the possibility of rocking the EU boat, conservative Ireland put its mouth where the money was and voted overwhelmingly for Maastricht.

Effectively, the EU gave conservative Ireland a stake in its own destruction. Would it have died anyway? Yes. Would it have died without a potentially disastrous struggle? Probably not. For when we look back over the last 30 years, the astonishing thing is not that there were sometimes bitter social tensions in the Republic but that they were contained with relative ease. With massive levels of unemployment and social exclusion, with a fierce struggle between secular and religious forces and with a violent conflict on its doorstep, Irish society should not have been able to accommodate huge economic and cultural changes. Without the EU's success in luring conservative Ireland into the modern project, it almost certainly could not have done so. That cultural shift lay behind the boom of the 1990s, like an undercoat of paint behind the glossy and often garish surface.

FEMINISTS AND BABY BOOMERS

One of the reasons the Irish as a whole got richer in the 1990s was that, as the decade wore on, there were progressively more people working outside the home supporting fewer dependants. Some of this shift came about for straightforward economic reasons: more people had jobs and fewer were unemployed. But much of it was due to a revolution in family structure influenced, to a very significant extent, by the rise of feminism. It worked in two ways. Married women joined the work-force in increasing numbers, or women postponed marriage and stayed at work, adding to the number of wage earners and boosting the availability of labour. And, both as a cause and a consequence of this change, the birth rate dropped suddenly and drastically, cutting the numbers of dependent children. That women had choices – and how they exercised those choices – was as important in the creation of the boom as any other factor. The progressive ideologies of the 1960s and 1970s were at least as crucial as the free market ideologies of the 1980s.

In most of Europe and North America, the baby boom followed the Second World War. In Ireland it came much later, after the First Programme for Economic Expansion. As late as 1970, Irish fertility was by far the highest of any country in the western, developed world. The total period fertility rate (TFR: the average family size of any woman based on what will happen if her current fertility rate continues over her child-bearing years) in Ireland was 3.87, compared to 2.41 for western Europe as a whole and 2.3 for central and eastern Europe. (Even this represented a decline from the peak of 4.1 in 1964.) Only Albania – the most isolated European nation – was more productive of children. For demographers, Ireland's birth rate was so far out of proportion to the rest of western Europe that it required "graphs to be rescaled to accommodate it".[7]

This meant that well into the 1990s, but especially in the 1980s, the Irish population was the youngest in the industrialised world, with 24 per cent of the population under 15 as late as 1996. (The EU average at the time was just 18 per cent.) Yet by 1994, the TFR in the Republic had halved to 1.87, below the level required to replace the population in the long run (generally taken as 2.1 children). The number of babies born in 1999 was 20,000 fewer than in 1980 – a drop of well over one-quarter.[8] The Irish had stopped breeding like rabbits and started breeding like Europeans.

Much of this underlying change was driven by the Left. In 1970, when the first Commission on the Status of Women was established, the importation and sale of "artificial" contraceptives was illegal, women in the civil service and in many white-collar private-sector jobs were obliged to resign their posts if they married and discrimination between men and women (and between married men and single people of both sexes) was open and pervasive.

Pressure from the Left, from the feminist movement and from the EU gradually dismantled these formal barriers. The Supreme Court overturned the total ban on contraceptives in 1973 (though, as late as 1991, the Virgin Megastore in Dublin was fined IR£500 for selling condoms to unmarried people and warned that it had "got off lightly"). The marriage bar in the public service was lifted in 1973, pay discrimination was proscribed in 1974, other obvious forms of discrimination in the workplace were banned in 1977 and the right to maternity leave was introduced in 1981.

As the effects of these changes gradually worked their way through, women began to take their place in the work-force. In 1983, Ireland had the lowest rates of married women's participation in the work-force in Europe. By 1997, about half of Irish mothers were active in the work-force, and Irish levels of female participation were coming close to the European average. The rate of female participation in the labour force in 1994 was just 39 per cent. By 1997 it had risen to 42 per cent and by the middle of 2000 to 47 per cent. This was still well below the EU average of 59.5 per cent in 1999, but the rate of improvement was nonetheless remarkable.

This dramatic shift in the nature of the Irish population had very significant economic consequences. In 1986, there were 22 dependants for every ten workers in the Irish economy. By 1999, there were 14 dependants for every ten workers. By 2011, assuming an unemployment rate of 5 per cent, there will be 11 dependants for every ten workers. The so-called dependency ratio will have halved in 25 years. You don't need to be an economist to realise that this underlying shift has huge implications for prosperity. More wage earners bringing in more income with fewer dependants to spend it on is an obvious formula for a consumer boom. Yet, in the anxiety to claim Ireland as a model of free market conservatism, it is conveniently forgotten that the Irish boom had mothers as well as fathers.

TRADE UNIONS

Whatever the merits and deficiencies of the social partnership process, few people who know any-thing about the Irish economy in the 1990s would deny that it had a huge role in the creation of the boom. The trade union movement was the key player in this process. Union leaders, with the support of their members, recognised that wage increases were being swallowed up by inflation and that an uncompetitive economy maintained mass unemployment. Their willingness to break this cycle by agreeing to six successive national pay deals in return for tax reform, the introduction of the minimum wage and some modest progress on social welfare payments was a crucial factor in generating and sustaining economic growth. The positive effects were so obvious that even those parties initially hostile to the whole notion of allowing trade unions such a prominent role – notably the Progressive Democrats – quietly dropped their opposition. Right-wing economists who wouldn't recognise a trade union if it danced naked in front of them don't like to mention this factor in the Irish boom but, whether the Heritage Foundation believes in it or not, it exists.

Despite the problems and limits of the partnership process – and there are many – it should be recognised that part of the motivation of the trade unions was a solid commitment to the old-fashioned socialist value of solidarity. While right-wing economic theory suggests that people act in the economy only out of a narrow sense of self-interest, the unions were also concerned with notions of fairness. They believed that by signing on to a national wage agreement the bargaining power of the powerful sectors – especially the public sector unions who could exert enormous political pressure by going on strike and creating immediate and profound disruption to vital public services – would be at the service of weaker, lower-paid workers. They also believed that they could protect those who depended on social welfare payments from the worst effects of the cutbacks in public spending. While it can be argued that their commitment to these ideals was weaker than it might have been or that it was less effective in practice than in theory, the existence of those values was a key element in the transformation of the Irish economy in the 1990s.

The reality of the Irish boom, then, is that it was a vastly more complex phenomenon than the crude simplicities of neo-conservative ideology would suggest. Some of the ingredients did come from what might be regarded as the official centre-right cookbook: low corporate taxes, wage moderation, fiscal responsibility. But others were supplied by the Left: an active State, public investment in human capital, feminism, international solidarity from the European Union, an intelligent trade union movement. What's more, the globalisation that Ireland was taking advantage of owed vastly more than is generally acknowledged to the values of the Left.

2

COPYRIGHT AND COPYLEFT

Everybody knows that innovation comes from the private sector. Individual entrepreneurs have great ideas. They battle through the obstacles placed in their way by banks, trade unions and governments. They succeed against all odds. Their hunger for private profit has beneficial side-effects for everyone. Jobs are created. New products and services become available. Wealth is spread around.

The extraordinary individuals who do all of this acquire the aura of mythic heroes. The blurb for the Ernst & Young Entrepreneur of the Year Awards provides a perfect summary of this process of deification and the ideology which fuels it:

> Everything seems to start with an entrepreneur. An innovative business model. The creation of new jobs. New industry trends. Throughout history, entrepreneurs have changed the economic and social landscape ... They see opportunity and seize

it. With sweat, determination and a lot of hard work, they fan sparks of imagination into the bright blaze of success. They are our finest and most important national resource.

These mythic creatures can be identified by their outstanding qualities: "They always have passion – they live and breathe their enterprise. They have an unshakeable confidence and enthusiasm that is contagious. They have laser-focus, creativity and discipline. They have perseverance and courage."

Much of this is sometimes true, of course. There are brilliant, passionate, creative and driven people who do make things happen in the business world. Any intelligent society will want to encourage and support such people. The problem, though, is that the idolatry requires a demonology on the flip side. The demon is the public sector: the State, the public service, all kinds of institutions that are not driven by the profit motive and therefore do not understand the primacy of greed in human affairs. These are the forces of darkness, good at using taxation to steal wealth from its creators and spending it on their pet schemes and projects but incapable of creating anything. Everything, after all, starts with an entrepreneur.

That all of this is nonsense ought to be obvious. Take a look at the list of winners of the Ernst & Young Entrepreneur of the Year Award in Ireland, the very jamboree that is advertised with the gushing prose just quoted. The first names listed are those of Denis O'Brien, for his work as head of the Esat Technology Group, and Moya Doherty and John McColgan for their huge success with the great Irish culture/business extravaganza, Riverdance. All three are undoubtedly passionate, driven, disciplined, risk-taking business people. All certainly proved extremely adept at making a lot of money.

But did Esat and Riverdance really "start with an entrepreneur"? Clearly not. Denis O'Brien made a huge fortune with Esat by getting a public resource from the State – Ireland's second mobile-phone licence – at a very low price, in circumstances which prompted a large-scale investigation by the Moriarty Tribunal, and then selling it on at a vast profit to British Telecom. Some of the elements of Riverdance were first assembled at one publicly funded institution, the Abbey Theatre, and the show itself was commissioned and launched into the stratosphere of international publicity by another public institution, RTÉ. At the time of Riverdance's invention, indeed, Moya Doherty was that terrible antithesis of the entrepreneur: a public servant, employed as a producer by RTÉ.

If this is true for the microcosm of globalisation that was 1990s Ireland, it is even more true on the larger scale of globalisation as a world-shaping process. The global economy as it is represented in Ireland is powered above all by two economic sectors: information and communications technology and biotechnology. These are the twin pillars of capitalism in the late 20th and early 21st centuries, and Ireland's ability to capture a disproportionate amount of foreign direct investment in these fields accounts for its economic success in the 1990s. By 2001, the dominance of industries related to computers and biotechnology was immediately obvious from a breakdown of Irish exports: 60 per cent of exports came from these two sectors (see Table 2.1).

Table 2.1 Components of exports 2001

Export	%
Chemicals and pharmaceuticals	34.9
Computer equipment	24.2
Machine and various equipment	16.8
Food, live animals	7.2
Miscellaneous manufacturing	12.9
Others	4.0

Source: Central Statistics Office, external trade March 2002

It is no exaggeration, therefore, to say that Ireland's boom was founded on the extraordinary innovations in computers, communication, biotechnology and medicine of the 1980s and the 1990s: the Internet, the World-Wide Web and the revolution in genetics whose pinnacle is the Human Genome Project. And all of these were public projects, developed primarily by public servants. None of them came from rugged individualism. On the contrary, each was made possible by a spirit and practice of co-operation in which insights and ideas were shared. None of them was fuelled by the profit motive. On the contrary, each was carried forward by people who did not hope to make a killing from their work.

THE INTERNET

The development of the Internet was an entirely public enterprise. The idea was envisaged by a public employee, J. C. R. Licklider of Massachusetts Institute of Technology (MIT), in August 1962. He imagined a globally interconnected set of computers through which everyone could quickly access data and programs from any site. He took the idea with him when he went to work for the US Defence Advanced Research Projects Agency (ARPA), which in 1973 initiated a research programme to investigate techniques and technologies for interlinking computer networks of various kinds. The next key development was the establishment by another US Federal agency, the National Science Foundation, of the NSFNET network to link computers in universities and scientific institutes. From there, other public networks were developed in the US and in Europe (the Cyclades network in France and the network developed by the British National Physical Laboratory being the most prominent examples), overwhelmingly by State and public institutions.

At every stage in this process, the key concepts were openness, sharing, collaboration. The whole notion of the Internet was rooted in the old-fashioned, much derided principles of communal property, co-operative working and public utilities. Right at the start, in MIT in the 1960s, the idea of what was initially called the "time-sharing computer system" was understood in this way by those who were bringing it into being. In 1966, Fernando Corbato and Robert Fano, who developed MIT's first computer network systems, wrote that:

> The time-sharing computer system can unite a group of investigators in a co-operative search for the solution to a common problem, or it can serve as a community pool of knowledge and skill on which anyone can draw according to his needs. Projecting the concept on a large scale, one can conceive of such a facility as an extraordinary powerful library serving an entire community – in short, an intellectual public utility.[1]

The scientists and engineers who were central to the development of the Internet have written that:

> A key to the rapid growth of the Internet has been the free and open access to the basic documents, especially the specifications of the protocols. The beginnings of ... the Internet in the university research community promoted the academic tradition of open publication of ideas and results ... The Internet is as much a collection of communities as a collection of technologies, and its success is largely attributable to both satisfying basic community needs as well as utilizing the community in an effective way to push the infrastructure forward.[2]

If ideas such as "an intellectual public utility" and "satisfying basic community needs" have been central to the Internet, the revolution in information technology went even further into traditional socialist territory as it became more sophisticated. The great genius of software development, Richard Stallman of MIT's Artificial Intelligence Laboratory, was motivated by a passionate belief that software programs should be public property.

Having emerged from a scientific culture in which computer codes were co-operatively written, freely shared and always regarded as being in the public domain, he was appalled when fellow researchers started to patent and copyright computer operating systems so that they could make big money from them. "I decided no way, that's disgusting, I'd be ashamed of myself. If I contributed to the upkeep of that other proprietary software way of life, I'd feel I was making the world ugly for pay."[3]

Stallman believed that users of a computer program should be free to study how it works, to share it with others and to improve it for the benefit of the public. He therefore pioneered a whole new notion of intellectual property. Software would be released into the public domain with a licence requiring anyone who redistributed it, with or without changes, to pass on the freedom to further copy and change it under the same conditions. To distinguish this new licensing system from the old concept of copyright, he called it "copyleft". Using this new concept, a young Finnish undergraduate, Linus Torvalds, developed what is generally acknowledged to be the best computer operating system, Linux.

The reason Linux is a better system than anything Microsoft has produced is copyleft. Because it is a free, open code, it is continually tested, debugged and improved by hundreds of thousands of users – many more than even a giant corporation such as Microsoft can possibly employ. Linux and the Apache web-server program — which is acknowledged as the best software for hosting web sites and which is also a copyleft product – demolish the myth that only the individual entrepreneur and the profit motive can create efficient innovation. Linux and Apache are not just expressions of nicer ideals than the programs developed for profit by large corporations. They are better.

The spread of this new technology from small, highly specialised professional élites to the wider world of human communication was also crucially influenced by communal, non-profit values. It was people, not profit, that turned interesting little developments into a technological and economic revolution. Nobody planned the phenomenal growth of Internet use. E-mail was developed by Ray Tomlinson almost as an afterthought to serious work, and even its inventors were taken aback at the critical role it played in the development of the Internet as a tool of mass communication. USENET, the system on which the development of chat groups was built, started out as a way of disseminating information about program bugs and fixes for users of the UNIX operating system. Yet "it turned out to be the medium via which an enormous set of global conversations on an unimaginable range of topics is conducted and around which a glorious diversity of virtual communities has flourished."[4] These conversations and communities, in turn, are a product, not of the marketplace, but of civil society. Voluntary organisations and campaigning groups were a key ingredient in the recipe that transformed a network of nerds into a huge global social and economic force.

The final stage in the information technology

revolution, the development of the World-Wide Web, followed precisely the same pattern. The World-Wide Web didn't emerge from the brain of a lone entrepreneur made feverish by visions of vast profits. It came from an altruistic public servant working for an international, publicly funded institution, the European Centre for Nuclear Research (CERN) in Geneva. It was the brainchild of Tim Berners-Lee, an English scientist. Berners-Lee could have made a fortune from his work, for, as John Naughton puts it, "This is a man who invented the future, who created something that will one day be bigger than all the other industries on earth. This is a man whose intellectual property rights could have made him richer than Croesus."[5] By inventing the World-Wide Web, Berners-Lee transformed the Internet from a resource for nerds into a part of daily life in the developed world and, incidentally, a whole new arena for commerce. Fortunes have been made from his invention, but not by him.

None of this is to suggest that private enterprise did not play a role in the information-technology revolution. Private companies did a superb job of inventing, manufacturing, marketing and distributing the machines (personal computers) that made the technology available to the masses. Without companies such as Apple and Data General and Intel, the transformation of computing power from a highly specialised and extremely expensive resource to a widely available and relatively cheap commodity would not have been possible. But it is equally true that the private sector on its own would never have invented the Internet in anything like its current form. This is not just a matter of speculation. At various stages, the scientists developing the computer networks actually tried to enlist the corporate world. The giant telecom corporation AT&T, which at the time controlled the long-distance telephone system in the US, turned down an offer to become involved with the development of digital computer networks in the 1960s on the basis that "First it can't possibly work, and if it did, damned if we are going to allow the creation of a competitor to ourselves."[6]

Even when the ARPA network was up and running in 1972, AT&T was offered the entire system on a plate. They looked at it in some detail and finally decided that it didn't have a future. Xerox worked on many of the same ideas at its famous Palo Alto Research Center and made many technological breakthroughs, but it failed to develop them because it did not see the prospect of making a profit. Even Bill Gates, the most successful and ruthless entrepreneur of the information age, missed the significance of the Internet. As late as 1995, in his book *The Road Ahead*, he was still not treating the World-Wide Web as a development of great import, mentioning it just seven times in nearly 300 pages of thoughts on the information highway.

The reality is that without the rather old-fashioned left-wing values of co-operative work, public property and the common good there wouldn't have been a booming IT sector to drive

Ireland's economic development in the 1990s. It was public institutions, public values and public funding that created the revolution. These institutions and values proved to be more effective, more efficient, more dynamic and more innovative than the private sector. Without them, the huge wave of investment in Ireland by Intel, Microsoft, IBM and so on in the 1990s would have been a much more modest trickle. The Irish boom owes at least as much to the values of the Left as it does to those of the Right.

THE HUMAN GENOME PROJECT

The values of the Left also played a large part in the other economic sector that created the investment and export boom: the medical, pharmaceutical and biotechnological industries. The biotech equivalent of the Internet is the Human Genome Project (HGP), the international consortium of public institutions that set out to map the entire human DNA sequence. This is a project of immense philosophical, cultural and political significance, laying bare as it does the raw material of common humanity. It has also, however, a huge economic dimension. The information gained in the mapping of the human genome is and will be the key to the development of new medicines. The development and manufacture of these products is bound to be one of the motors of economic development in the 21st century. The achievement of the HGP is by any standards a great work of economic innovation, and the Irish pharmaceutical and biotech sectors depend on it for much of their vitality.

And this, too, is a product of public institutions and values. The work was done by public employees at publicly funded universities and laboratories. More starkly, the whole project was surrounded by an explicit clash of traditional right-wing and left-wing ideals. In the race to map the genome, the ethos of private enterprise and private greed went head to head with the ethos of public enterprise and the common good. The result should have scotched forever the myth that the pursuit of profit necessarily generates greater efficiency, better work and ultimately more public good than the supposedly sclerotic and ineffectual workings of public institutions.

The HGP was established in 1990 as a publicly funded, collaborative international effort committed to the principle that all its information would be freely available to the scientific community. This principle had two sources. One was the obvious reality that the human genome is literally common property. It belongs to us all in the most direct sense. The other was that free availability of the data would actually be more productive and efficient. Making sense of the sequence of three billion elements will take a very long time and no single institution or company could possibly muster the resources to do it. Making the sequence public property meant that anyone with expertise and ideas could contribute to the project.

This monumental breakthrough for humanity as a whole was, however, very nearly wrecked by private enterprise. In 1998, a commercial company, Craig Venter's Celera Genomics, launched itself with the stated aim of becoming "the definitive source of genomic and associated medical information". Had it succeeded, the human genome would have become private property, protected by patent and available only to those who were willing and able to pay for it. Aside from the moral and social consequences of such a development, it would also have massively retarded the economic potential of medical biotechnology by confining the scope for discovering and developing new products to a small and secretive élite.

The power of the prevailing orthodoxy is such that it was widely taken for granted that a private company working for profit would inevitably be cheaper, more effective and faster moving than a public consortium. Venter announced that his budget would be just a tenth of the $3 billion that the HGP would cost, and this figure was taken as gospel in most media reports. In fact, what Venter was proposing was a much cruder project than the HGP. He would produce a rough draft of the sequence using a fully automated mechanical procedure. The HGP, on the other hand, was about producing a complete detailed sequence, which involved much more meticulous human work. Its budget also included a wide variety of other genetic projects, including the development of new technologies and databases. Nevertheless, as Francis Collins, head of the National Human Genome Research Institute in the US, put it, "the public project was portrayed as labouring with a clumsy, bureaucratic, difficult-to-implement strategy, and these fast-moving folks in the private sector were going to run circles around us …"[7]

What would in fact have emerged from Venter's profit-driven operation would have been a map of the genome detailed enough to allow for the patenting and privatisation of this common property, but that still would have required many years of work to close an estimated 100,000 gaps and correct potentially catastrophic errors. But the notion that private enterprise must be better placed enormous political pressure on the HGP. By October 1999, when Venter's Celera operation applied for patents on 6,500 human genes, the possibility of the genome becoming private property was very real. By early 2000, Celera launched its first public share issue and raised almost $1 billion – a clear sign that the stock market expected vast profits to flow from these patents.

What saved the HGP was, at least in part, the idea of copyleft. It became clear that Celera, for all its grandiose claims, was in fact using the publicly available data generated by the HGP as the framework for its own discoveries and was positioning itself to be able to charge others for using it. The HGP's head of sequence analysis, Tim Hubbard, was directly influenced by what the copyleft movement had done in the field of information technology, and though the HGP was legally unable to make its data available on a similar basis, it did manage to uphold the ideal. By sticking to its guns and continuing to work on co-operative principles, the HGP succeeded in publishing a draft sequence for the entire human genome in February 2001. It also rescued the idea of independent science from looming catastrophe.

The patenting of genes remains a threat, however, and attempts to exploit public work for private gain continue. In March 2000, for example, a company called Hume Genome Sciences was granted a patent on a human gene called CCR5. When it applied for the patent it didn't know what the cell actually did, and this presented a major problem for its application. Publicly funded scientists then made the important discovery that CCR5 is one of the gateways through which HIV enters cells. Armed with this knowledge, the company was then able to confirm the role of CCR5 through experiments and thus to get its patent. The public discovery of the gene's function makes it potentially crucial in the fight against Aids. Yet that same discovery has been abused to make the gene valuable private property. Researchers can't work on it without paying large licence fees.

Yet the success of the HGP, like the development of the Internet and the World-Wide Web, was a triumph for public values and for the principles that have always informed socialism. Sir John Sulston, the British geneticist who drove the HGP forward and fought to protect its underlying integrity, has written that:

> I'd thought of the Human Genome Project as being an uncluttered and altruistic activity, but it became embroiled in a rapacious struggle for wealth and power. I was forced to realise that in our society one can get into trouble for giving away something that can make money.[8]

Yet he continues to argue that scientific data such as the genome sequence is public property and uses language that would have been familiar to socialist campaigners in the first half of the 20th century. He writes that "to the extent that the data are fundamental and important, they should be available to all on equal terms, not to the wealthy few". He says, quite bluntly, that "greed nearly succeeded in privatising the human genome, our own code, and indeed remains a threat to it". He stands up for "the commonality of the ever-growing body of knowledge and the need for it to be freely available to all".[9]

Between them, the Internet and the Human Genome Project represent the benign face of globalisation. One has made virtually instant global communication available to hundreds of millions of people, especially but not exclusively in the developed world. The other is reminding us, in the most profound way, that we belong to one species, one indeed that has a far narrower range of genetic differences between individuals than any other comparable species. And these two forces are also at the heart of Ireland's new economy.

What we need to remember is not that their development teaches us a simple lesson that the public sector is good and the private sector is bad. Many public institutions do bad things and many private companies contribute enormously to the sum of human happiness. The lesson, rather, is that private companies and lone entrepreneurs do not have a monopoly on productive innovation.

Not only did many of the brightest and the best innovators who have shaped the 21st century work for motives other than private gain (the esteem of colleagues, the prestige of high achievement and the sheer fun of making something new), but also values that we can only call socialist have been utterly crucial to the success of those enterprises. Contrary to the orthodox clichés, much of the leading-edge commercial development of the late 20th and early 21st centuries has not been built on the foundation of private greed. On the contrary, it would have been impossible without the values of the Left.

And this in turn raises a series of questions for Ireland. A process of development that owes so much to public ideals will be self-defeating if it erodes the very basis of those ideals. If the message we take from the boom is that communal values are redundant, and that the profit motive has triumphed, the Celtic Tiger will eat itself. If we forget that private enterprise is exploiting possibilities opened up by public values, we will deplete the very resources that will be crucial to the survival of a prosperous society.

3

FISCAL RECTITUDE

In April 1989 the then Taoiseach, Charles Haughey, flew back into Dublin Airport from a trip to Japan. While he was in Tokyo, he had come across one of the more exotic aspects of eastern culture, the pending resignation, in the face of a financial corruption scandal, of his counterpart, Noboru Takeshita. Such things, of course, could never happen in Ireland.

Charles Haughey did, nevertheless, have some political worries on his mind. His minority Fianna Fáil administration was facing defeat in the Dáil on a private members' motion put down by Brendan Howlin of the Labour Party. This pesky affair concerned an electorally insignificant group of people: haemophiliacs who had contracted HIV from blood products supplied by the State. The bothersome motion called on Haughey's government to put up all of IR£400,000 to form a trust fund to help these sick and desperate citizens.

The Fianna Fáil leader made it clear that he would not stand for this kind of nonsense. Public spending was being cut back ferociously and there was no money for hard cases. In front of members of the opposition, who subsequently claimed never to have witnessed so vehement an attack, he launched a verbal onslaught on his senior colleagues for failing to prevent this ridiculous embarrassment. Although his followers loyally obeyed his orders to vote against the haemophiliacs, the motion was carried by 72 votes to 69. Haughey took this so badly that he called a general election.

In the same week that Charles Haughey was facing down the importunate haemophiliacs, his bag-man, Des Traynor, approached Ben Dunne's accountant, Noel Fox, and asked for UK£150,000 to top up previous gifts from the same source of almost UK£600,000.

By a coincidence so gruesome that it would be unacceptable in a work of fiction, the chairman of the Blood Transfusion Service Board, the agency that supplied the haemophiliacs with the infected blood products, was the same Noel Fox.

The following week Haughey called the then chief executive of the VHI, Tom Ryan, into his office and let it be known that the State health-insurance agency should cough up IR£57,000 for an operation for a Government minister, Brian Lenihan.

Shortly after that, in the space of just two months, Fianna Fáil collected IR£200,000 – half of what was intended for the entire haemophiliac community – from business leaders to pay for Mr Lenihan's medical expenses.

The general election called to show the virtues of fiscal rectitude was an interesting time for two of Haughey's senior colleagues. In the weeks after they voted against the trust fund, Ray Burke lodged IR£107,000 to his bank account and Pádraig Flynn received IR£50,000 from the property developer Tom Gilmartin. Between them, Haughey, Burke and Flynn received more money in personal donations in the run-up to that election than the trust fund voted for by the Dáil would have given the haemophiliacs.

In the same month that Haughey called that election, April 1989, the financier Dermot Desmond concluded an agreement with the liquidator of the Johnston Mooney and O'Brien bakery to buy its Ballsbridge, Dublin headquarters for IR£4 million. The sale to a company called Chestvale was concluded on September 1st 1989. Just six weeks later, Dermot Desmond told his bankers, Ansbacher, that he would be selling the site to a UK property company for IR£5.8 million. This deal was not done, however, because Dermot Desmond had become involved in negotiations to sell the site to a public company, Telecom Éireann.

On January 9th 1990 Dermot Desmond told Telecom that the "best price" he could get the site for would be IR£9.4 million – well over twice what it had cost three months previously and IR£3.6 million more than he was willing to sell it for two months previously. Telecom agreed to pay this price. Essentially, Dermot Desmond and a small group of associates made over IR£5 million in less than a year at the expense of the public.

It is generally agreed by conservative commentators that the stringent fiscal policies of Charles Haughey's Governments after 1987, the control of the current budget deficit and the slowing of the growth in the national debt contributed significantly to the emergence of the economic boom later on. The era when Charles Haughey's cronies were doing the rounds of the rich businessmen was also the time when the Republic was undergoing a traumatic adjustment to the hard realities of the global economy.

One of the myths of the Irish boom is that the cutbacks in State spending worked so well because there was a social consensus that the pain should be shared. We are told in a World Bank discussion paper, for example, that "The pain of the stabilization was made transparent and spread across all groups but with protection for social welfare."[1]

In fact the pain of stabilisation was borne by the weak (children in schools, the sick in hospitals, the disabled) and by the heavily taxed PAYE sector of the economy. The well-off evaded taxes on a massive scale.

The question we have to ask is: was it entirely coincidental that the pain of that adjustment was visited disproportionately on the weak and the poor? Was it chance that while old people were lying for days on hospital trolleys because wards had been closed, some businessmen were receiving extraordinary largesse from the State? That while primary schools were falling apart, no serious effort to correct the public finances by actually collecting taxes from the very rich was ever made? That even when a major Irish company such as Goodman International was caught evading its tax responsibilities, which it actually admitted, no one was brought to book?

Those questions are not academic inquiries about the past. They relate directly to one of the most pertinent facts of Irish life in the early years of the 21st century: that the gains are not being shared by those who took, and continue to take, the pain.

Until we understand the choices made in the course of Ireland's final entry into the global economy in the late 1980s and early 1990s, the nature of contemporary Irish society is incomprehensible. Until we know why some were given a leg up into the roaring 1990s while others were kicked in the face, we won't be able to come to terms with the coexistence of manic affluence and mean despair in boom-time Ireland.

The biggest, but sometimes least obvious, present-day consequence of corruption is the nature of that economy itself. One of its outstanding features, and one of the main causes for anxiety about its future, is the extraordinary degree to which it depends on external investment. Or, to put it another way, the extraordinary degree to which it has not been driven by Irish entrepreneurs.

There are many reasons for that failure, but the cosy relationship between a small golden circle of native business people and some key members of the political élite is certainly one of them. Nothing discourages enterprise more than the belief that the system is crooked and that rivals with an inside track already have it sewn up. Nothing stifles innovation more effectively than the easy availability of nice little earners, accessible through the simple application of monetary grease to the wheels of the political gravy train.

Long before the Irish political landscape was dominated by tribunals of inquiry into the corrupt practices of the 1980s and 1990s, Irish people understood quite well that they lived in a democracy where influence and power could be bought.

It's worth looking back on an MRBI poll conducted for an RTÉ *Today Tonight* programme produced by Mary Raftery in November 1991. To the proposition that "there is a Golden Circle of people in Ireland who are using power to make money for themselves", a massive 89 per cent agreed. Eighty-one per cent agreed that the people in this Golden Circle were made up in equal measure of business people and politicians. Seventy-six per cent thought the scandals that were then beginning to emerge "part and parcel" of the Irish economic system rather than one-off events. Eighty-three per cent thought that the then current scandals were merely "the tip of the iceberg", while 84 per cent said business people involved in corrupt dealings and fraud got off more lightly than other criminals. Significantly, the figures for Fianna Fáil voters were, in general, only slightly lower than those for supporters of other parties.

In November 1993 Maurice Doyle, then the governor of the Central Bank, gave a talk to the Philosophical Society at Trinity College Dublin on the subject "Recession – Is There a Way Out?" He had decided to speak out on matters of public policy, among them "the high tax burden imposed on labour". He was concerned that "the PAYE sector shoulders a disproportionate burden of income tax". He felt that there was "ample scope for the income tax net to be further widened" so that the burden could be spread more evenly.

But he was also worried about "the sizeable black economy in Ireland". He pointed to the activities of those he referred to as "fraudsters". The wrongdoers he targeted were bogus welfare claimants drawing the dole but "defrauding the system". He suggested that there were much larger numbers of these criminals than the public realised and that the 2 per cent fraud rate indicated by a Department of Social Welfare study might be "only the tip of the iceberg". And he spelled out what he felt were the damaging social effects of such crimes. He thundered:

> Apart altogether from the question of fraud and the amount of money involved, the example set to the rest of the labour force by those who work and also draw the dole is corrosive of any spirit of enterprise in the community … Greater vigilance is required … and those who do not actively seek work should not receive the welfare entitlements they are currently afforded.
>
> These comments may not be "politically correct" but they have to be made.

This was the authentic expression of the official

mind. Maurice Doyle was one of the most distinguished members of the public service, a man who had been, before being elevated to the Central Bank, secretary of the Department of Finance.

He was addressing real and immediate political concerns, seeking to explain to the population in general why income tax was so high and what could be done about it. He wanted to raise the spectre of the black economy, of cheats, of fraud. But to him, it seemed, the black economy was about fellas doing nixers. The cheats were chancers turning up at the dole office every week with their pockets bulging with under-the-counter cash payments. The fraudsters were shifty members of the underclass, up to every trick in the book, giving a bad example to the honest, decent workers.

We now know from his evidence to the Dáil Committee of Public Accounts inquiry into the massive evasion of Deposit Interest Retention Tax (DIRT) in the 1980s and early 1990s that the Central Bank, which Maurice Doyle headed, was well aware that there were many other "fraud-sters" who were "defrauding the system" by evading tax through bogus non-resident bank accounts. In 1986, for example, the Central Bank was told by Allied Irish Banks that "up to £600 million of non-resident deposit accounts may be misclassified i.e. they were deposits from Irish residents".

In April 1991 the group financial director of AIB told the Central Bank that "AIB had a contingent liability amounting to some hundreds of millions of pounds virtually going back to the introduction of DIRT."[2]

The people who were using these bogus accounts to defraud the Revenue, and the banks which facilitated their crimes, were respectable and well-off citizens, setting a bad example for the labour force. Their actions clearly had an important impact on the public finances, on tax equity and on many of the other areas that the governor of the Central Bank addressed in his speech.

But Maurice Doyle did not call in their case for greater vigilance to prevent the compliant taxpayer from being defrauded. On the subject of this kind of fraud he, and the official élite to which he belonged, were inclined to silence.

This silence is eloquent, for it tells us more than any torrent of words about the assumptions that have shaped the Ireland we now inhabit. In the painful process of adjusting the Irish economy to the demands of the global marketplace, there was no room for doubt about who should bear the pain: the old people lying on trolleys in hospital corridors, the children in damp, overcrowded classrooms, the so-called Ryanair generation of young emigrants who had the good grace to feck off to America when the élite declared, "We can't all live on a small island."

While they were to see the stern face of State austerity, their betters were to get off scot-free. All through the years in which boom-time Ireland was being formed, what might – for want of a better word – be called the Establishment made sure that three basic ideas became part of the consensus. There is not much money in Ireland ("We are", as Charles Haughey admonished us, "living beyond our means"). The crisis in the public finances is entirely about public spending. The worst parasites are dole scroungers and welfare cheats.

Each of these was demonstrably untrue. There was a lot of money around but much of it was hidden in bogus accounts. The current budget deficit was out of control, not just because the State was spending too much but also because it was failing to collect vast sums that it was owed. And the big cheats were large farmers, shopkeepers, business people – pillars of the community.

Even the official tax figures issued by the Revenue Commissioners showed that there were vast amounts of uncollected taxes. In 2002, arrears in payments totalled 3 per cent of tax revenue – a fairly reasonable figure. In 1988, however, arrears (totalling IR£4.4 billion) stood at an astonishing 37 per cent of tax collected. In other words, for every IR£2 collected by the Revenue, there was IR£1 that they knew to be owed but that was uncollected. Even as late as 1996, the figure stood at 11 per cent.

Unofficially, however, there was, as the State well knew, widespread tax evasion by the well-off. A tax amnesty in 1988 allowed long-term evaders to declare their incomes without paying penalties and to pay only a fraction of what they owed. Large-scale abuse continued, however, much of it at the very top of Irish society. The Taoiseach, Charles Haughey, was a participant in the Ansbacher (Cayman) tax scam, a sham discretionary trust structure which allowed wealthy individuals to claim that their money was invested offshore when it was in fact available to them in Ireland.

The Central Bank knew about the scam but accepted assurances by the scheme's mastermind, Des Traynor of Guinness and Mahon (G and M) bank, that the amount of so-called loans extended to Irish residents was being run down even though the Bank knew that new loans were being granted and new deposits received. References in an internal Central Bank report, as early as 1976, to Ansbacher's "tax evasion", an illegal activity, were doctored to refer to "tax avoidance", which is legal.[3] A report two years later revealed the existence of so-called loans to a director of the Central Bank itself, Ken O'Reilly-Hyland, backed by a deposit in Ansbacher Cayman. Nothing was done.

Especially after the end of 1979, when Haughey became Taoiseach, the rise in the amounts of money held by the scheme in Dublin is spectacular. In April 1979, the deposits stood at just under UK£5 million. Three years later, they had reached almost UK£27 million. By then, the Cayman operation, initially a sideshow, had become larger than its parent company.

This may be mere coincidence, but it is striking that the Central Bank's scrutiny of G and M became far less inquisitive after Haughey's assumption of the leadership of Fianna Fáil. At a review meeting in April 1981, there was, as the Ansbacher Inspectors' report puts it, "some passing reference to particular loans with a

Cayman connection" but "no further discussion of the overall nature of this banking activity or of its taxation implications". These evaders were people who lived in two worlds, a public one of official politics and religion and a private one of pure materialism. A fascinating detail in the appendices to the Ansbacher report, for example, is the way Denis Foley, Fianna Fáil TD for North Kerry until the general election of 2002, made his money in the 1960s and 1970s. By day, he collected rates and rents for Tralee Urban District Council. By night, he booked bands for the Mount Brandon and Central hotels. By 1979, when he became an Ansbacher customer, he had accumulated IR£30,000 from this extra job. This was a lot of money in those days, and it seems puzzling that the job could have been so lucrative. Denis Foley's statement, however, clears up the mystery. He was being paid twice. The hotels paid a fee, of course. But he also charged the bands what he calls "commission" for the privilege of being booked.

Many of the Ansbacher élite were shaping the world that Irish people live in, not just metaphorically but also literally. John Byrne's Cayman Island trusts held some of the properties that dominate central Dublin: O'Connell Bridge House, Ballast House, D'Olier House, Hawkins House. Arthur Gibney and Sam Stephenson, who are also named in the report, designed and developed huge monuments to the new Ireland, including, perhaps appropriately, the Central Bank. One of their big projects, the redevelopment of Fitzwilliam tennis club, was enabled by Ken O'Reilly-Hyland and

AFTER THE BALL

Liam McGonagle, both of whom are named in the report.

Large parts of modern Dublin, especially in and around Ballsbridge, were built by G&T Crampton, who engaged in joint ventures with G and M. The proceeds of one large development were placed in six Cayman trusts. And, of course, the very materials used in all of these developments were often supplied by CRH, eight of whose directors at one time or another were clients of Ansbacher.

These people, in other words, were in the business of literally creating the reality of modern Ireland. They were used to the notion that what people saw around them could be transformed by an act of will. You could tear it down, put something else in its place and, if necessary, front it with a mock-traditional façade. If you could shift the physical world around you, how hard could it be to shift money around?

This power to define reality, and to get every-one who mattered to agree with you, is what made the Ansbacher operation possible. The alternative reality – that respectable business people might be engaged in criminal behaviour – became unthink-able, unsayable and inconceivable. Since a criminal was a thin-faced, ratty-looking kid in white socks waiting outside the District Court, soft-spoken bankers could not possibly be criminals.

Meanwhile, the abuse of non-resident accounts was an open secret throughout the banking industry in the 1980s and 1990s. The banking industry facilitated people who were known to be residents in claiming that they were non-residents to avoid paying DIRT. The 1999 report of the Dáil Committee of Public Accounts into the scandal found that there was a particularly close and inappropriate relationship between banking and the State and its agencies. "The evidence suggests that the State and its agencies were perhaps too mindful of the concerns of the banks and too attentive to their pleas and lobbying," the report says.

Bogus non-resident accounts were breaches of exchange control but the Central Bank, despite its responsibility to defend the exchange rate and protect the integrity of the Irish currency, took no action. According to the report:

> The Central Bank had an inappropriate and outmoded approach to supervision, given the growing sophistication of banking and the changing role of banks in society ... There was an insufficient concern with ethics and supervision other than from the standpoint of a traditional and narrow concern with prudential supervision in the Central Bank.

The mixture of political corruption and conservative ideology that created and sustained this culture of tax evasion had huge long-term effects. It encouraged large sections of the Irish business class to salt away its disposable capital in unproductive offshore or bogus non-resident accounts rather than to invest it productively. It contributed to a fiscal crisis in which there was no option but to slash State spending on social programmes. This in turn meant that those who needed help were left to fend for themselves while those who had money were able to improve their relative position in society. While ordinary working people were paying tax at up to 60 per cent, many people with considerable resources were able to avail of amnesties at a rate of 15 per cent or to evade tax altogether. When the boom came, the rich were in an even better position to benefit from it.

Even in direct fiscal terms, the decision to stabilise the public finances by cutting social programmes rather than by collecting the taxes owed by the wealthy has proved expensive in the long term. The worst of the cutbacks, for example, were in the health system. A massive 3,244 beds were closed in public hospitals between 1987 and 1989, a reduction of almost 20 per cent. A further 13 per cent of the bed capacity was cut by 1993. In the eastern region, where all the main national hospitals are located, there was a 29 per cent reduction in bed numbers. Beds also went in psychiatric and geriatric institutions.[4]

The legacy of all of this was still being felt in 2003. The boom years were haunted by the chaotic state of the public health service, and the taste of wealth was embittered by the persistence of hospital conditions that sometimes reeked more of squalor than of affluence. And trying to do something about it even with the abundant resources available in the late 1990s proved enormously difficult and immensely expensive. Pouring resources into the wasteful, inequitable and chaotic system left behind after the devastating cuts of the late 1980s was a deeply problematic exercise. Fixing the health service will now cost far more than was saved by attacking it so crudely in the first place.

4

POVERTY AND INEQUALITY

In July 2003, the annual United Nations Development Programme's flagship *Human Development Report 2003* was launched in Dublin. It was quite a diplomatic triumph for the Irish Government to have this highly important document unveiled in its capital, with the Taoiseach Bertie Ahern and Bono taking the limelight. The party was somewhat spoiled, however, by the uncomfortable fact that the report's Human Development Index ranks Ireland second lowest in the western world, just ahead of the United States, for poverty and inequality.

The roll of honour and dishonour, ranking countries for a combination of poverty and inequality, is called the HPI-2 index. The higher the rank, the better the country is doing.

There are many reasons for Ireland's miserable performance, and the socially unjust society we inhabit has been a long time in the making. It is, however, sustained quite deliberately by a political policy of keeping both taxes and social spending low.

HPI-2 ranks for 17 selected OECD countries

1. Sweden	10. Japan
2. Norway	11. Italy
3. Finland	12. Canada
4. Netherlands	13. Belgium
5. Denmark	14. Australia
6. Germany	15. United Kingdom
7. Luxembourg	**16. Ireland**
8. France	17. United States
9. Spain	

A recent CORI Justice Commission analysis compared Ireland's tax take with that of our fellow European countries. It showed that, following Budget 2003, Ireland's tax take remains the lowest in Europe, an outcome that applies irrespective of whether the calculations are performed using GDP or GNP. Ireland's tax take stands at just 27.7 per cent of GDP and 33.9 per cent of GNP. (Sweden is highest at 53.2 per cent; France is at 46.4 per cent; Italy at 41.8 per cent; Germany at 36.4 per cent and the UK at 37.4 per cent.) These figures suggest that Ireland's taxation rate is at least 7.5 percentage points below the EU average of 41.44 per cent. Worldwide only three other OECD countries collect less tax than Ireland: these are Korea, Japan and Mexico. Even the United States, at 29.6 per cent of GDP, is almost 2 per cent higher than the corresponding Irish figure.[1]

The other side of this shiny mirror is, inevitably, a shabby social infrastructure. As well as having the lowest taxes, Ireland also spends the least on social protection.[2] The percentage of GDP spent on social protection in 2000 (the latest year for which Eurostat has statistics) was highest in Sweden (32.3 per cent), France (29.7 per cent) and Germany (29.5 per cent). The EU average is 27.3 per cent, and no country spends less than 20 per cent. Except, that is, Ireland, which spends a spectacularly low 14.1 per cent. We spend, in other words, less than half the proportion of our national wealth looking after the old, the disabled and the ill than Sweden, France or Germany does.

Just as significantly, the proportion of GDP spent on social protection declined steadily throughout the boom years. In 1991 it was 19.6 per cent; in 1993, 20.2 per cent; in 1996, 17.8 per cent; in 1998 15.5 per cent; in 1999, 14.8 per cent and in 2000, 14.1per cent.[3] The pattern since the mid-1990s is unmistakable and it is not accidental. A coherent policy of limiting social spending has been in place. Given that every percentage point in the national tax take represents in Irish terms about €1.1 billion for the Exchequer, an Irish Government raising average European levels of tax would have at least an extra €8 billion a year to spend on the sick, the old, the disabled and the poor. When politicians boast of Ireland's low taxes, what they really mean is that we should be proud of not spending this money to help citizens who need it.

Ireland's shameful standing in the UNDP index is underpinned by these policies. It makes us very good at producing two things that we don't package and sell: poverty and inequality.

POVERTY

The most up-to-date data available on poverty in Ireland comes from the 2000 Living in Ireland Survey, conducted by the ESRI. Using a poverty line of 50 per cent of the average household income (which means, in 2003 terms, someone living on less than €174.74 a week for a single person) the findings reveal that at the height of the recent period of the boom one in every four households and one in every five people in Ireland was living in poverty (see Table 4.1).

Table 4.1 Percentage of households and persons below relative income poverty lines for 2000

% line	Households	Persons
40	11.8	9.9
50	**25.8**	**20.9**
60	32.9	28.3

Source: Nolan et al., *Monitoring Poverty Trends in Ireland*, ESRI, 2002

These levels of poverty got worse in the course of the boom. In 1994, 17.4 per cent of Irish people were living on less than half the average income. By 2000, that had risen to 20.9 per cent. This deterioration in relative income poverty has a simple explanation. Average incomes rose sharply during the economic boom, fuelled by increases in income from work and property, and median incomes were pulled up by the growing proportion of people in employment; this raised the income thresholds below which people are deemed to be in relative income poverty. For example, the money value of 50 per cent of mean weekly household equivalent income increased by 75 per cent between 1994 and 2000 (from IR£64.69 to IR£113.22) and by 21 per cent between 1998 and 2000 alone. Once increases in social welfare were not of the same magnitude, some increase in relative income poverty was certain.

A somewhat different measure of poverty is given by eight indicators used in ESRI studies to indicate "consistent poverty":

- a meal with meat, chicken or fish every second day
- a warm, waterproof overcoat
- two pairs of strong shoes
- a roast joint of meat or its equivalent once a week
- new, not second-hand, clothes
- going without a substantial meal
- going without heat
- going into debt for ordinary living expenses

In the period 1994–2000, the percentage of people unable to get one or more of these necessities dropped from 9.0 per cent to 6.2 per cent. The most frequent experiences of deprivation were: going into debt for ordinary living expenses (5.6 per cent of households); depending on second-hand clothes (3.3 per cent of households); lacking a roast or its equivalent once a week (1.9 per cent of households); and going without heat (1.8 per cent of households).

These measures are pretty crude, however. Poverty is about far more than income, or even access to material goods. It is also about work, educational opportunity, parenting, access to culture, a feeling that you have the right to part-icipate in and influence your society. It is about feeling reasonably secure. And, in this regard, the risk of falling into poverty is an important factor in misery and happiness.

Since 1994 every household type, except for the unemployed who already had a high risk, has seen its risk of falling into poverty increase (see Table 4.2).

Table 4.2 Risk of falling into poverty of persons below 60% of median income by labour force status

	1994	1997	1998	2000
Employee	3.2	4.7	3.0	7.4
Self-employed	16.0	14.4	17.2	20.8
Farmer	18.6	16.7	24.6	24.3
Unemployed	51.4	57.7	58.9	50.7
Ill/disabled	29.5	52.5	54.5	54.4
Retired	8.2	13.5	19.0	33.8
Home duties	20.9	32.6	44.6	47.6
All	15.6	18.2	20.0	22.1

Source: Nolan et al., *Monitoring Poverty Trends in Ireland*, ESRI, 2002

What is especially striking about these increases

is that a substantial number of households headed by an employee are at risk of poverty. The simple formula used by Governments in the last ten years – that employment is the way out of poverty – is not by any means the full truth. That there are many working families living in or near poverty is evident not just from the figures but also from the payment of the Family Income Supplement (FIS), a social welfare measure specifically for families headed by a worker. In 1999, 14,549 families were receiving the FIS; in 2000, 13,062; and in 2001, the latest year for which figures are available, 11,570. These families contained 26,426 children. In the case of 3,833 of these families, their income from work was less than IR£200 per week.

None of this is abstract. Being poor means that you are under constant pressure to make ends meet. An examination of low-income families was published by the Vincentian Partnership for Social Justice in 2001.[4] It analysed the experiences of families dependent on social welfare and jobs at minimum wage rates. The study concluded that "these rates do not reflect the current cost of even the most frugal standard of living. There is an urgent need to increase them to a realistic level at which people can live with some dignity and without the burden of a continuous shortfall."

The study involved 118 people in 12 community centres in 7 parts of Dublin city completing a detailed questionnaire on their weekly income and expenditure. It found that housekeeping and food were the most costly items for the majority of households regardless of income. It also showed that people on social welfare experienced short-falls due to the inadequacy of their income rather than the bad management of their income. The resulting financial pressure diverted family attention away from allocating enough time, commitment or money to areas such as education. Consequently children may even leave school early to avoid further financial pressure on their parents.

This kind of stress is not easily represented in statistical data. An eloquent snapshot, however, is provided by a Dublin City Council study of the tenants on its housing estates in 2001.[5] It shows a large majority having trouble keeping up with their rent (see Table 4.3). With just a third of rents fully paid up, it means that for many families, even at the height of the boom, the wolf was at the door.

Table 4.3 Status of rent account 2001

Rent account status	Number of tenants	%
Fully paid up	7,980	33.1
In arrears of 1 to 3 weeks	7,816	32.5
In arrears of 4 to 6 weeks	2,489	10.3
In arrears of over 6 weeks	5,788	24.0

INEQUALITY

Poverty is not just about individuals or even families. It is also about areas. Urban Ireland is socially segregated and poverty tends to be concentrated in specific places. This creates a kind of informal social apartheid. Again, the 2001 Dublin City Council study gives a striking indication of the concentration of poverty in working-class estates. It suggests that, in the boom years, while Ireland as a whole remained deeply unequal, some became even more unequal than others.

The average weekly income of all individuals aged 18 years and over accommodated by Dublin City Council stood at €165.50 in 2001. In 2001 the average income of a household accommodated by Dublin City Council was €313.24. This is much less than half the national average household income for the 1999/2000 period which was €666.96.

The impact of these lower incomes on poverty is obvious. It means that the local authority tenants were vastly more likely to be poor than the general population (see Table 4.4).

Table 4.4 Dublin City Council general tenant households and Irish population 2001

	Tenants	General pop.
% less than 40% of average income	39.2	9.1
% less than 50% of average income	62.5	20.4
% less than 60% of average income	73.1	27.2

The proportion of City Council tenant households with incomes below 50 per cent of average was 4.3 times higher than the general population. The proportion of City Council tenant households with incomes below 60 per cent of average seems to have fallen only slightly in the boom years. In 1994, 77 per cent of urban local authority tenants in Ireland had incomes below this level. By 2001 this had dropped to 73 per cent. However, the proportion of Dublin City Council tenant households that have incomes of less than 50 per cent of average actually grew very sharply. In 1994, 51 per cent of urban local authority tenants had incomes below this level. In 2001 in Dublin the figure was 62.5 per cent.

In general, the gap between rich and poor had been rising in Ireland since the mid-1970s. The boom years did nothing to change the trend in any significant way. The clearest picture of what happened is provided by the Household Budget Survey published by the Central Statistics Office in 2001. It covers most of the boom years, the period when money was rolling in. The average gross weekly household income for the State in 1999–2000, at IR£525.06, was 53 per cent higher than the IR£343.14 recorded five years earlier. Yet this period of profound change actually made the gap between the rich and the poor worse. A person in the lowest 10 per cent (decile) of earners saw his or her disposable income rise in those five years by 33.3 per cent. A person in the top decile saw her or his income rise by 61.8 per cent. The average disposable income of households in the top 20 per cent (with a gross weekly income in excess of IR£800.66) increased by over 61 per cent over the five years, compared with 37 per cent in the bottom 20 per cent (with a gross weekly income below IR£168.90).

The average disposable income of households in the lowest income decile was IR£83.67 compared with IR£1,125.22 in the highest income households. Thus the ratio of the highest to the lowest household incomes was approximately 13 to 1 in 1999/2000 compared with 11 to 1 in 1994/1995.

This resulted to a significant extent from the Government policy of not allowing social welfare payments to grow as fast the general economy. In 1992, social welfare spending was 12.3 per cent of Irish GNP. In 2001, it was just 8.2 per cent.[6] Even more pointedly, however, overall budgetary strategy actually redistributed income towards the better off.

Since 1997, the impact of the budgetary policies pursued by the current Government has been to further increase income inequality. This is revealed by a CORI Justice Commission analysis of the last six budgets which shows a dramatic widening of the rich/poor gap as each of the six budgets gave substantially more to those who were better off than to those who were poorest in Irish society.[7] Overall, this gap has now widened by €276 a week.

Like poverty, inequality is about more than money. It shapes access to crucial parts of the public world, in particular education and health.

Education

Ireland likes to think of itself as a witty, literate and learned society. It sells itself to tourists with the images of great writers. It collects Nobel prizes for literature. But it is also a country with shocking levels of illiteracy. At the start of the 20th century, about 12 per cent of the Irish population was regarded as illiterate. Now, a century on, the OECD International Adult Literacy Survey published in 1997 found that 23 per cent of those tested do not have the literacy skills necessary to function in contemporary society.

They scored at the lowest of five possible levels, one of which involves being able to locate a single piece of information in a text where there is no distracting information and when the structure of the text assists the search. The 23 per cent of Irish people mentioned in the survey includes both those who can do only this kind of task and those who can't. Therefore, some of those included in this figure are in fact falling below the lowest level measured. More than half the Irish people surveyed were in the lowest two levels of literacy, with just 13.7 per cent in the highest category.

On average, 54 per cent of the State's adults are below the minimum level of literacy, with almost 23 per cent at the lowest level of literacy. Only Poland had a higher percentage below minimum literacy levels.

More than 60 per cent of Irish adults at the lowest literacy level had left school without Junior Cert. qualifications.

In spite of the massive disadvantages faced by these citizens, participation in adult education in Ireland is also among the lowest in the OECD countries. Just over 20 per cent of adults participate in adult education, half the international average.[8]

Even though public expenditure on higher education has increased substantially over the last decade, rising from just under €400 million in 1991 to just over €1,400 million in 2002, access to third-level education in Ireland, and in particular to university, remains astonishingly unequal. The most recent statistics from the Higher Education Authority (HEA) show that the sons and daughters of professionals are over 15 times more likely to enter college than students from lower socio-economic groups. According to the figures, only 159 students from a household headed by an unskilled manual worker entered university in 2001–2002. In sharp contrast, more than 2,400 students from a higher professional background registered.

In 2001, the country's biggest university, UCD, had 8,354 students from professional, employer and managerial backgrounds. It had 937 from semi-skilled or unskilled backgrounds. The National College of Art and Design had no one at all from an unskilled manual background. University College Cork had 4,034 students from professional, employer and managerial backgrounds and all of 162 sons and daughters of manual workers. Trinity had 4,291 students whose parents were professionals, employers or managers and 95 whose parents were manual workers.

For all the public money that has gone into higher education in the 1980s and 1990s, little has changed in this regard. The improvements in social equity are extremely slight, even in a period when the university sector was expanding very rapidly. The rate of admission to higher education in 1998 was 44 per cent, more than double the rate for 1980 of 20 per cent. But in the boom years, the proportion of full-time undergraduates who came from unskilled manual backgrounds actually fell. In 1990–1, it stood at 3.3 per cent of the total. In 2000–1, it was just 2.9 per cent. At the other end of the socio-economic spectrum, the higher profess-ional group had a 97 per cent participation rate in higher education.

Even when students get similarly low exam results, those from professional backgrounds have a greater chance of progressing to third level. For example, only 9 per cent of students from unskilled backgrounds with four passes get to third level, whereas 30 per cent of those with the same results from a higher professional family reach college.

In Dublin, five of the districts in the south of the city have admission rates in excess of 50 per cent, ranging from 77 per cent in Dublin 18 to 56 per cent in Dublin 16. Only one district in the north of the city has a rate in excess of 50 per cent – Dublin 15 at 54 per cent. For example, in north inner-city Dublin only 17 young people managed to make it to third level. This compares with 336 in Foxrock/Glencullen and 481 in Terenure/Rathmines.

The divisions are not purely geographic, though. They exist at school level too. Seventy-one per cent of those in fee-paying secondary schools get to college, compared to 50 per cent of community schools and 38 per cent of vocational schools.

In some respects, in the boom years things got worse, not better.

When Professor Patrick Clancy published

figures for participation in third-level education in 1992, there was widespread concern at the following third-level participation rates: 21 per cent in Finglas/Ballymun and 19 per cent in Clondalkin/Neilstown. But in his 2002 report, which reflects the situation in 1998, participation in these areas of Dublin had actually declined. Finglas/Ballymun had a third-level participation rate of 14 per cent, with the Clondalkin/Neilstown area slipping back to 13 per cent.

Even when working-class students do get to university, there is still an obvious social division in that the children of higher professionals, managers and employers continue to dominate the most prestigious and potentially lucrative courses. Courses which provide access to the professions – medicine, law, veterinary science and dentistry – remain dominated by children of higher professionals, many of whom work in these areas, according to another HEA report.

The introduction to the report by the chairman of the HEA, Dr Don Thornhill, states: "The more prestigious the sector and field of study, the greater the social inequality in participation levels."[9] Children of higher professionals and employers make up more than 55 per cent of those taking law courses, for example, compared to 0.5 per cent from unskilled backgrounds and 3.1 per cent from semi-skilled backgrounds.

In this way, access to education both mirrors and sustains social inequality. The most recent OECD study – *Education at a Glance*, 2002 – shows that the career earnings potential of graduates is significantly enhanced, with a third-level education delivering an annual earnings premium of 57 per cent in Ireland. Being well-off almost guarantees that you will get to university and getting to university almost guarantees that you will be well-off.

Health

As a general rule, poorer people are less healthy than richer people. Though Ireland's health system is extraordinarily bad at keeping records of the social background of the people it treats, the big picture is pretty clear.

- In 1996 unskilled manual men were twice as likely to die as higher professional men.
- In 1996 unskilled manual men were eight times more likely to die from an accidental cause than higher professional men.
- In 1996 you were almost four times as likely to be admitted to hospital for the first time for schizophrenia if you were in the unskilled manual category than if you were a higher professional.
- In the early 1990s the babies born to unemployed women were over twice as likely to have a low birth weight as babies born to women in the higher professional group.
- People in the "unskilled manual" socio-economic group have worse health than professional groups in all years and for all the conditions which have been analysed.

- There was a 3.4-fold difference in the age-standardised death rates between men in the lowest and the highest socio-economic groupings during the period 1989 to 1998.
- In 2001, life expectancy at birth for Traveller men was 9.9 years less than for settled men and 11.9 years less for Traveller women than for settled women.
- Adults in the lowest socio-economic group were twice as likely to report a long-standing illness as those in the highest socio-economic group.[10]

All of these suggest that the poor have the greatest need of access to the health service and ought to find it easier to get treatment. In fact, the opposite is the case. In 2002, public spending on health was €8.3 billion, almost a quarter of current Government spending. This money comes from general taxation, yet it underpins a system that, if public patients were black and private patients were white, would lead to universal international condemnation of an apartheid system.

Ireland openly operates a two-tier health system, in which those who can afford to pay generally get immediate or quick access to hospital treatment, while those who can't often face very long waiting lists

Private treatment is not really private. Private insurance has been and continues to be promoted through a range of public subsidies. These include tax relief on premiums – initially at the taxpayer's marginal rate, but this has been reduced to the standard rate in stages between 1994 and 1996. This change, combined with the general reduction in tax rates, has reduced the individual value of this relief as a share of the premium. However, it still cost €94 million in 2002. Retention of this relief is stated Government policy. There is no tax relief for voluntary health insurance in Belgium, Denmark, Finland, France, Sweden and the United Kingdom and only very limited tax relief in Germany and the Netherlands.

In addition, the cost of private claims and thus insurance premiums has been deliberately kept lower than would otherwise be the case by applying below-cost charges for private accommodation and services in public hospitals. One of the main findings of a recent study of this issue is that the charges levied may only cover around half the direct cost of private provision. The rest of the tab is picked up by the taxpayer.

This policy is quite deliberate. As far back as the 1980s, it has been obvious that equality of access depends on a common waiting list for treatment. The Commission on Health Funding, which was set up in June 1987 and reported in September 1989, envisaged the continuation of the system of allowing private practice in public hospitals but argued that the potential for unequal access inherent in these arrangements should be directly addressed:

> It is inequitable that patients in medically similar circumstances do not have equal access to services. As a result, unnecessary frustration and suffering is caused to those on long waiting lists. To overcome this problem, we recommend the introduction of an

objective system of assessment for access to publicly funded hospital services. This would relate to
all planned admissions, whether to public or
private accommodation, and would result in a
common waiting list from which cases would be
taken in order of medically established priority
rather than the type of accommodation sought.

The idea was that access to public hospitals
should be based on objective assessment of
medical need. This idea was explicitly or
implicitly rejected by successive governments.

The boom did little to end the misery of public
patients waiting for treatment. The total number
of adults waiting for more than 12 months
increased between 1996 and 1999, with very sharp
increases in 1997 and 1998. In 2000, there was a
very sharp fall in the overall total. Nevertheless,
the number of adult long-waiters was 26 per cent
higher in 2000 than in 1996. There were fewer
long-waiters in only two specialties: cardiac
surgery, where there was a dramatic decline, and
orthopaedics, where there was a modest one.
Exceptionally large increases occurred in ear, nose
and throat and plastic surgery.[11]

Even after very large increases in public
funding for the health system, and the emergency
treatment of thousands in private hospitals paid
for by the State, hospital waiting lists dropped by
just 157 people between September and December
2002. According to the Department of Health, at
the end of December 2002, 29,017 people were
waiting for treatment. The figures showed that at
least 5,000 adults had been waiting for a minimum

of one year for treatment. However, since a number of hospitals did not specify how long people had been waiting for certain types of treatment, the reality could be significantly higher. At least 1,000 children had also been waiting for a minimum of six months.

The impact of the waiting-list crisis varied from hospital to hospital, with Dublin faring worst (see Table A.1, p. 170).

Table 4.5 Waiting lists for public patients by treatment required, mid-2003

Specialty	Adults:		Children:	
	3–12 months	over a year	3–6 months	over 6 months
Cardiac surgery	166	93	8	6
ENT	1103	1293	339	828
Gynaecology	805	456	0	0
Ophthalmology	2499	563	82	99
Orthopaedics	2170	1214	35	83
Plastic surgery	651	976	111	460
Surgery	1562	1061	175	454
Urology	792	675	12	37
Vascular	755	1148	0	0

Source: irishhealth.com, Waiting List Watch

All of this contributes to Ireland's having the highest premature mortality rate of all EU countries. Irish life expectancy, at 65 years, was the lowest of all 15 EU countries in 1997. Death rates from heart disease and cancer are extremely high by EU standards. The general death rate from heart attacks in Ireland is 176 per 100,000 of population, compared to 108 in the EU as a whole. In those under 65, the death rate from heart attacks is nearly double the EU rate: 46 per 100,000, compared to 25 in the EU as a whole.

Treatment for cancer is often astonishingly poor for a wealthy, developed society. Less than one-third of the 12,000 patients who require radiotherapy in the Republic each year receive it. Public patients face a three-month delay for radiation treatment that they have been told is both necessary and urgent. The first five-year analysis of cancer trends by the National Cancer Registry of Ireland, published in February 2002, showed that 50 per cent of patients with lung cancer received no cancer-specific treatment and 57 per cent of those with leukaemia were not offered chemotherapy. Two-thirds of patients in the Republic with last-stage stomach cancer received no cancer-specific treatment.

Regional variations in the availability of radiotherapy have a particular impact on poorer patients, since they make it necessary for many cancer-sufferers to travel long distances and stay away from home for long periods. The Republic's two radiotherapy units are based in Dublin and Cork, so while 39 per cent of patients nationally have radiotherapy for breast cancer, only 24 per cent of those living in the Western Health Board benefit. Nor are things likely to get much better in the immediate future. The budget of St Luke's Hospital in Dublin, the only specialist cancer hospital in the State, was cut by €1 million in 2003.

The reality is clear: wealth and poverty in Ireland are matters of life and death. And the lives of the poor are worth much less than those of their betters.

5

ON THE OUTSIDE

The tide of social change that created and
sustained the boom swept some parts of Irish
society along with it. But as it recedes, many are
left with a set of unfulfilled promises. For all its
new openness, the Republic is still marked by
systemic discrimination.

CHILDREN

In the mid-1990s, Ireland had the highest rate of
child poverty in the EU. The situation did improve
somewhat in the late 1990s, but by 2000, one in
four Irish children (270,000 boys and girls) was
still living in a household where the annual
income was less than 50 per cent of the average
disposable income. At the height of the boom in
2000, between a quarter and a third of Irish
children, depending on the measure of poverty
used, was experiencing deprivation.

Income alone, however, may not be the best
measure of child poverty. The crux in a society

where life chances are ever more strongly deter-
mined by formal schooling and qualifications is
educational opportunity. And in this regard the
situation is brutally clear: there are thousands of
children who are already massively diminished
before they enter adulthood.

Perhaps the most astonishing evidence of
official neglect is that no one actually knows how
many children never make it to a second-level
school at all. Given that the legal school-leaving
age is 16 (and/or three years of second-level
schooling), this is in itself extraordinary. It is all
the more scandalous because the best estimate of
the National Economic and Social Forum is that a
thousand children a year fall into this category.[1]

Over the period 1980–1996, the number leaving
secondary school with no qualifications fell from 10
to 4 per cent of the cohort. This progress seems to
have essentially stopped in the boom years,
however. In 1999, the year for which the most up-to-
date statistics are available, almost 13,000 young
people left before completion of the Leaving
Certificate, of whom 2,400 or 3.2 per cent left with
no formal qualifications. While the data show a
significant percentage drop of nearly 20 per cent
between 1996 and 1999 for those leaving without a
qualification, it is important to emphasise that, in
absolute terms, there has been a small increase. This
group, moreover, is even more marginalised now
than in the past because of "qualifications inflation":
the more young people there are with high
qualifications, the worse off are those with none.

For specific groups, the inability to complete

second-level schooling is even worse. In 1999, 4.1 per cent of males (relative to 2.5 per cent of females) left school without qualifications. Social class has an even bigger influence: the percentage of students from an unskilled manual background who left with no qualifications (9.1 per cent) contrasts with less than 1 per cent from the higher professional, lower professional and salaried employees groups.

Socio-economic differences are also evident among those who left school having completed the Junior Certificate only. Just over 25 per cent of the unskilled manual group left with a Junior Cert., while the figures for the employers and managers, higher professional and lower professional categories were 8.2, 7.7 and 5.6 per cent, respectively.

The impact of all of this on the subsequent careers of the young people involved is stark. Over 40 per cent of those who left with no qualifications were unemployed in 1999 compared to just 3.4 per cent of those who completed Senior Cycle – a set of figures that is likely to be far worse in the poorer economic conditions of post-boom Ireland. Conversely, levels of entry into higher professional jobs are higher among more qualified leavers. For example, almost 10 per cent of those with Leaving Certificates enter the banking sector, compared to only 1 per cent of those with Junior Certificates. Of those without qualifications, none are working in the banking sector. In the industrial sector, those without qualifications account for 47 per cent compared with 39 per cent who have the Leaving Certificate.

Educational attainment is thus strongly linked with earnings. Recent figures for school leavers illustrate that those who left school unqualified receive an average hourly income of €5.75. This rises to €6.07 for those who leave after Junior Certificate. Those who left school having completed the Leaving Certificate earned €6.13 per hour on average. Even these disparities probably understate the long-term consequences, as someone leaving school with no qualifications or with a Junior Cert. only is more likely to end up in a dead-end job where there is little prospect of promotion.

In terms of how the State treats children, the disparities in educational opportunity mean that it spends far more on the strong than on the weak. The State invests only €20,000 in a child's primary education over eight years. It pays €25,000 to get the same child to Junior Certificate. It spends €60,000 on every student who gets a university degree.[2] So the child who does not make it to secondary school or who leaves after Junior Cert. is given far less public money than the child who gets a degree. Unless, of course, he or she graduates to prison, in which case the State pays €100,000 per year to keep him or her in jail.

In this regard, there is no more eloquent signal of the State's priorities than the condition of many primary schools in one of the richest nations on earth. A survey by *The Irish Times* of 62 out of 137 primary schools on the Department of Education's emergency repair list as of May 2003 revealed slum conditions: outdoor toilets, faulty electrical

systems, sewage problems, unsafe playgrounds
and severe restrictions on space.[3] Some of the
lowlights included:

- *Charleville NS, Tullamore, Co. Offaly*: The
  200-year-old school has been condemned.
  Prefabs were put in 30 years ago as a
  temporary solution. The school received
  funds for emergency electrical repair
  work, completed in January at a cost of
  €3,000. A new school was promised in
  1998 but the school was never told when
  this would materialise.
- *Scoil Chuimín, Oughterard, Co. Galway*: The
  roof on the 63-year-old school fell in on a
  teacher and is constantly being repaired.
  They have been waiting nearly six years
  for a new roof. There are puddles in the
  halls. They got electrical sockets at
  Christmas 2002 under a minor works
  grant. There is no space for resource
  teachers, a library or a computer room.
  Woodworm is rampant.
- *Gallbhaile NS, Galbally, Enniscorthy, Co.
  Wexford*: Pupils have not been able to
  drink the water for the past 10–15 years as
  it is contaminated. The Government has
  been paying for supplies of Ballygowan
  bottled water.
- *Lettergesh NS, Renvyle, Co. Galway*: The
  principal was promised, in September
  2002, a playing field, new toilets in the
  classrooms, new windows and doors, a
  larger Portakabin for the resource teacher,

a new heating system and rewiring. All of this has now been taken away except for the heating system. There are no circuit breakers on the old fuse board, which the school cannot afford to replace.

- *An Cloiginn, Cleggan, Co. Galway:* The school has outdoor toilets, no space for a resource teacher, asbestos in the ceiling. It has been granted €40,000, which is €30,000 short of what is needed.
- *Kilconly NS, Co. Kerry:* Before Easter, the sewage system leaked onto an adjoining property and this leak was fixed. However, the school needs another classroom, a resource room, a staff room, new toilets, a new roof and a new sewage system. It has got planning permission since February 2002 but has no money.
- *Ballinahinch NS, Birdhill, Co. Tipperary:* The septic tank has been leaking for the past year, but funding to fix it was withdrawn last Christmas.
- *St James NS, Bantry, Co. Cork:* A new school was promised six years ago after the Southern Health Board condemned it. The roof leaks. The girls' cloakroom doubles as the school office, a learning-support room, a meeting room and an inoculation room if a doctor has to visit. There is no hot running water. There are three sinks and only one cold tap can be running at a time. The toilets have no heat or light. The windows don't open or close and a

double-glazed door has been installed to keep out rats and mice. There is no central heating. Instead, storage heaters and three dehumidifiers are running constantly.

- *St John's Girls and Infant Boys School, Limerick:* There is scaffolding around the school to prevent stones from walls falling on children's heads. Pipes are exposed in the 60-year-old school.
- *Ballyroan BNS, Rathfarnham, Co. Dublin:* Pupils and teachers have to walk through the yard in the rain to get from one classroom to the next because there is no corridor. There are no fire escapes and no *en suite* toilets. They have been waiting since 1997 for a new school but had to settle for replacing rotten windows and doors. A health-and-safety/fire assessment has condemned the school as inadequate. There is no room for new teachers, so special-needs pupils have to be taught in the classroom surrounded by other children.
- *St Joseph's BNS, Terenure, Co. Dublin:* Sixty children who need resource teaching have to be taught in the corridors.
- *CBS, Francis St, Dublin:* Emergency grant aid was given to the school last February because it had no water. Water had to be delivered by the fire brigade.

Those children who are most at risk are still failed by the system. The Department of the

Environment's Assessment of Homelessness for 2002, published in May 2003, counted 1,405 children in homeless families. In addition, according to the official Youth Homelessness Strategy document (2001) there are 588 children who had left home and were without families. A Focus Ireland study of young people who had left the care of health boards at the age of 18 found that within two years an astonishing 68 per cent had been homeless at some point during that period and that 25 per cent had spent time in the juvenile justice system.

International research has shown that social background has a dramatic effect on a child's performance. At 22 months old, a very bright baby from a poor background does much better in tests than a slow child from a rich background. The bright child scores 85 points on the scale, the slow child 10 points. By the time the two children are three years old, however, their scores have almost converged – 55 to 45. At the age of six, the lines cross, and the rich, slow child passes out the poor, bright child. From then on the lines continue to move in opposite directions.[4]

All this gives the lie to the neo-liberal line that wealth is a product of individual endeavour and talent. In reality, those born into poor households have the dice loaded against them from the start. To put it at its most benign, these children have to show far more talent, courage and endeavour simply to achieve what more privileged children can take for granted. To put it more bleakly, if the achievement of a decent job and a comfortable existence is a race, these children start out a mile behind their competitors.

WOMEN

Since women played such an important part in the Irish boom, they became more visible in the public world. Ireland had two women presidents in a row and a woman Tánaiste. The first female editor of a national newspaper, Geraldine Kennedy of *The Irish Times*, was appointed. So was a woman Ombudsman. Women were more prominent in the workplace. Young women were more assertive, less demure and allegedly more hedonistic. With all of this going on, it was inevitable that some parts of the media would rush to declare the end of feminism. Some indeed, such as *The Irish Times* columnist John Waters, asserted that it was now men who were the victims of gender discrimination. Women had taken power and they were using it against men.

Such assertions are, at the very least, premature. Gender equality has made significant progress. But the idea that equality has actually been achieved is ludicrous. The 2003 UNDP Human Development Report ranks Ireland a poor 16th on its Gender-Related Development Index (GDI), among the lowest rankings for an OECD country.

More telling is the relationship between Ireland's status as a highly developed society on the one side, and the status of women as represented in the overall Human Development Index (HDI) and the relative position of women as represented by the GDI on the other. Normally these two indices should tell the same story, as the position of women is almost invariably better in the best-developed societies. By subtracting the GDI ranking from the HDI ranking, you can get a good picture of where a country's record on gender equality lies in relation to what it ought to be, given its level of overall development.

On this test, Ireland scores spectacularly badly. Its score is minus four, the same as the notoriously sexist Japan and with Japan the lowest of the 35 richest countries in the world. The facts behind this poor performance are stark.

Politics, civil service and law

Ireland ranks 59th out of 120 nations in the world when it comes to women's parliamentary representation. That puts Ireland lower than the European average (17 per cent), lower than the average for the Americas (16 per cent), lower than the Asian average (16 per cent) and on a par with the average for sub-Saharan Africa (13 per cent). The percentage of women elected to the Dáil has risen by only 1 per cent, to 13 per cent, over the past ten years.[5] It has taken ten years for the percentage to increase by even this pitiful amount. If nothing is done about this, it will take 370 years (10 years for each 1 per cent increase) for the Dáil to have an equal number of female and male TDs.

- As of mid-2003, there are 22 women serving as TDs. Ten counties do not have any women TDs. Almost 45 per cent of serving women TDs come from politically active families and have inherited their seats from their fathers, grandfathers or uncles. Women not belonging to politically active families form only 7 per cent of the current Dáil. Of the political parties, only Labour and the Progressive Democrats have anything approaching gender balance in their parliamentary parties.

Table 5.1 Situation of women TDs: election 2002 results

Party	Men	Women	% Women
Fianna Fáil	74	7	9
Fine Gael	29	2	6
Labour	14	7	33
Progressive Democrats	4	4	50
Green Party	6	0	0
Sinn Féin	5	0	0
Others	12	2	14
Total	144	22	13

Table 5.2 Situation of women senators: Seanad Éireann, 2003

Party	Men	Women	% Women
Fianna Fáil	25	5	17
Fine Gael	14	1	7
Labour	3	2	40
Progressive Democrats	3	1	25
Other	1	0	0
Independents	4	1	20
Total	50	10	17

Source: *Irish Politics: Jobs for the Boys*, National Women's Council of Ireland

- The number of women appointed to the Cabinet decreased by 7 per cent for the 2002 Government, while the number of women appointed as Ministers of State declined by a full 11 per cent.
- The percentage of women elected as local councillors remained unchanged at 15 per cent in the 1991 and 1999 local elections. South Tipperary and Westmeath County Councils each have a female membership of just 4 per cent.
- Nine per cent of secretaries-general in the civil service in 2001 were women.
- Seven per cent of high court judges in 2001 were women.

State boards

The percentage of women appointed to State boards has rarely reached 40 per cent, although this has been an official guideline since 1991 (see Table A.2, p. 172).

The percentage of women on State boards in the scientific, technological and industrial arena has actually fallen over five years and remains well below the 40 per cent target.[6] Women represent only about 25 per cent of those sitting on scientific, technological and industrial boards, 15 percentage points off the target, according to a study carried out by Women in Technology and Science (WITS) in 2003. The numbers on these boards were also falling rather than rising. A sample of 20 State boards in these areas showed an average 28 per cent of women board members in

1997 compared to 25 per cent in 2002, the group claimed (see Table 5.3).

Table 5.3 Women on scientific, technological and industrial boards

State board	% Women:	
	1997	2001
Aer Lingus	25	8
Aer Rianta	0	11
Bord Bia	40	20
Bord Gáis	0	12
Bord Iascaigh Mhara	17	17
An Bord Pleanála	33	42
CIÉ	17	37
Coillte	22	11
Food Safety Authority	44	20
Forfás	10	25
Health and Safety Authority	45	27
Higher Education Authority	37	37
IDA	25	17
Irish Blood Transfusion Service	50	50
The Medical Council	28	21
NCCA	41	17
National Roads Authority	43	36
An Post	13	21
RTÉ	44	50
Teagasc	18	18
Average	27.6	24.8

Business and employment[7]
The EU Commission Enterprise Scoreboard rates

Ireland the lowest in Europe for female entrepreneurs as a percentage of total entrepreneurs.
The information on women running small and
medium enterprises (SMEs) also places Ireland at
the lower end of the European scale. There is a
75/25 split in favour of men according to the
European Observatory for SMEs.

Aside from the question of equality, this is a
serious economic drawback. According to the
National Foundation for Women Business Owners, the number of women-owned firms is increasing at nearly twice the national rate in the US and
Canada. Ireland's very small female-owned
business sector suggests that it is missing out on a
significant area of economic growth.

- Women account for 30 per cent of new
  business start-ups across the EU. The
  majority of these are smaller than average,
  concentrated on the services sector and
  focused on local rather than export
  markets (European Observatory for SMEs,
  1996). Enterprise Ireland survey data
  indicate that just 15 per cent of
  manufacturing and internationally traded
  service projects in Ireland are promoted
  by women.
- Irish women's total manufacturing earnings are 66 per cent of male earnings in
  the sector.
- The cost of childcare in Ireland amounts
  to circa 20 per cent of the average
  industrial wage compared to an EU
  average of 8 per cent.[8]

- Eighty-one per cent of part-time workers are women.
- Of administrative, executive and managerial positions in Ireland, 73 per cent are held by men and 27 per cent are held by women. In contrast, 80 per cent of clerical positions are held by women.
- Thirty-six per cent of women are familiar with information and communications technologies compared to 64 per cent of men
- Labour force participation of women with dependent children in the 25–29 age group rose from 49.7 per cent to 52.6 per cent between 1994 and 1997. However, mothers of two children were 4.4 per cent more likely to leave the labour force in 1997 than in 1994, indicating the possible impact of the increasing cost and unavailability of childcare.
- Sixteen per cent of women in employment work in the manufacturing sector compared with 23 per cent of men. Eighty per cent of women work in services compared with 49 per cent of men.
- Seventy-seven per cent of women in employment work in four occupational groups – clerical workers (25 per cent), professional and technical workers (24 per cent), service workers (18 per cent) and shop assistants (10 per cent). These occupations account for 27 per cent of men.

- In 1998, women were 3 per cent of managing directors.
- In 2002, women were 13 per cent of Dáil representatives.

According to the ESRI report *How Unequal?*,[9] the gender wage gap stands at 16 per cent. Women's lower incomes and their generally shorter working-life span lead to lower pension entitlements. This is highlighted by the fact that, according to figures from the Department of Social, Community and Family Affairs in 2001, almost two-thirds of those in receipt of old-age contributory pensions are males whereas almost 60 per cent of those in receipt of old-age non-contributory pensions are females. When pension and health insurance entitlements are taken into account, the gender pay gap is close to 20 per cent.

The composition of the 10 per cent of Irish households with the lowest income shows many more women than men (61 per cent and 39 per cent respectively).

GAY MEN, LESBIANS AND UNMARRIED COUPLES

Since the repeal of draconian anti-homosexual laws in 1993, Ireland is at the forefront of countries that protect lesbian, gay and bisexual people against discrimination. There is now a strong set of laws protecting lesbians and gay men from discrimination inside and outside the workplace. Ireland's legal regime, however, is almost exclusively negative: it does quite well at proscribing discriminatory behaviour. What remains absent is any positive official, statutory and legislative recognition of same-sex partnerships. Few of the rights, responsibilities, commitments and benefits assigned to married heterosexuals are available to same-sex couples. Most are not available to non-married heterosexuals either.

Marriage for gay men and lesbians is not an option, yet marital status impacts significantly on rights in relation to pensions, residency and property. Since 1984, for example, all public servants, married or not, must contribute equally to a specific "spouses and children" pension fund, from which payments are made. No payments, however, can be made to an unmarried partner or to any children of that partner. Trustees of private pension funds can and sometimes do extend "relevant benefits" to same-sex partners and their children, but this is discretionary and there is no clear entitlement. When married couples separate or divorce, pensions are normally still partially allocated to the ex-spouse. No such rights accrue to non-married partners. The same discrimination is evident in inheritance law. Legal spouses inherit tax-free benefits, but same-sex partners ("strangers" in law) face two taxes: capital acquisitions tax (CAT) on the capitalised value of the pension and income tax on the pension itself. When a tenant dies, it is only when her or his partner is a joint tenant that the partner succeeds to the tenancy; in other cases, it will be very difficult to succeed to the tenancy.

Parental leave is a statutory right for the

biological parents of a child or for both adoptive parents, who must be a married couple. An unmarried partner of either a biological parent or of a parent who has an adopted child does not have this entitlement.

A legally valid marriage has tax advantages, but these are not available to a same-sex relationship which has no legal standing in the tax system. Joint assessment is not available to same-sex partners and neither partner can transfer their marriage allowance or avail of the double-rate tax band. In cases where only one partner in a same-sex couple is working, she or he will be taxed on a single-rate tax band. Gifts between partners are subject to tax, unlike married couples who are also exempt from stamp duty and from almost all probate tax on the transfer of any assets.

There is no guaranteed right of a same-sex partner to legal guardianship or custody rights over a natural or adopted child of her or his partner. The absence of adoption rights or guardianship rights means that a child has no automatic right to continue in a relationship with their second parent should their biological or legal parent become incapable of caring for them through death or serious illness.

A same-sex partner does not have any right, under Medical Council guidelines, to have any input into treatment decisions of seriously or terminally ill patients. Those rights are restricted to the legally defined next of kin. Funeral arrangements are the responsibility of the executor of the deceased's will. If the deceased has left no will, or has not made her or his partner the executor in the will, an unmarried partner has no rights.

All persons from the European Economic Area (the EU plus Norway, Iceland and Liechtenstein) can live and work in Ireland. When an Irish person wishes to bring her or his non-EEA partner to live or work in Ireland, immigration policy is weighted heavily in favour of married couples. Although non-EEA spouses do not have automatic rights of residence and work, the rules ensure that barriers are rarely put in place.

Same-sex partnerships, however, are ignored, and applicants are treated as single immigrants. The same applies to the right to Irish citizenship.

All of these areas are the direct responsibility of the State. While no Government can completely prevent all discrimination against lesbians and gay men – bullying in the schoolyard, for example, can be outlawed but never entirely obliterated – the law can be changed to make them full and equal citizens.

TRAVELLERS

In 1995, the Government-commissioned Task Force on the Travelling Community issued a comprehensive report with recommendations covering almost every area of Travellers' lives. In 2001, a progress report on the implementation of the recommendations found that there had been no real improvement. The failure, during a period of abundant resources, to better the lot of a relatively small community (24,000 people or 0.6 per cent of the population) that has suffered naked exclusion is perhaps the most damning indictment of boom-time Ireland.

The progress report found that 25 per cent of Travellers (6,000 people) were living in "very poor conditions". In 2001, 24.5 per cent of Traveller families (at least 5,000 people) were living on unserviced sites or by the side of the road. Unserviced sites have no regular refuse collection, running water, toilets, bath or shower, access to electricity, fire precautions or safe play areas for children. Since 42 per cent of the Traveller population is under 15, there are at least 2,000 children living by the roadside.

Traditional camping areas have been blocked off in most areas of the country with boulders, low studded walls and muck heaps designed to keep Travellers from camping in areas. This has severely affected Travellers' health. There is little doubt that their living conditions are probably the single greatest influence on their health status. Traveller women live on average 12 years less than women in the general population and Traveller men live on average 10 years less than men in the general population.

Very little progress has been made on meeting the needs of Travelling families for a decent standard of accommodation. According to the Housing (Traveller Accommodation) Act of 1998, 2,200 new halting-site bays were to be provided by 2004. As of December 2002, just 129 had been provided. Between 1995 and 2001, just 115 Traveller families were accommodated in group housing and 642 in standard housing.[10]

In fact, the whole strategy for Traveller accommodation has been fatally undermined by the Housing (Miscellaneous Provisions) Act, enacted in July 2002, which criminalises trespass on public and private land. The gardaí, on foot of a complaint, can now move on Travellers who are waiting for accommodation within local authority areas. Instead of providing accommodation for travellers in their area who are on waiting lists, local authorities can now simply force them out of the area.

The Irish Traveller Movement conducted a telephone survey from the period August 2001 to August 2002 and found that 471 families had been served with notices to move on without being offered any alternative accommodation.

IMMIGRANTS AND ASYLUM-SEEKERS

The boom made Ireland, for the first time in modern history, a country that attracts immigrants. It did not however end emigration. This created a kind of double vision in which migration appeared both as "us" (emigrants leaving and returning) and as "them" (foreign-born people coming to live in Ireland).

In the year to April 2002, the number of immigrants to Ireland was 47,500. Thirty eight per cent of these people, however, were Irish-born people returning to the country from abroad, reducing the real number to 29,450. Taking out immigrants from other EU countries and from the USA (who tend not to come to mind when people think of immigrants), there were just over 15,000 immigrants from the rest of the world. This is in fact fewer than the number of Irish people who emigrated to other countries in the same period: 18,800.

Most of these immigrants were used to fuel the boom, providing both highly skilled workers for the high-tech industries and people willing to do the jobs that the Irish no longer wanted – farm labour, poorly paid work in service industries – or could no longer supply in sufficient numbers – nurses and doctors for the public health service. Yet most experienced direct racism. Amnesty International's "Racism in Ireland: The Views of Black and Ethnic Minorities" found that 79 per cent of ethnic minority members had experienced racism or discrimination. (The figure includes Travellers and Irish-born black people.)

Many of these racist incidents were not one-off occurrences. Asked "How often if at all have you heard or seen people making insulting comments about your skin colour, or ethnic background, including the way you dress?" 36 per cent said "frequently". Over 44 per cent of the abuse took place on the street, 24 per cent in shops and 23 per cent in pubs.

For asylum-seekers, however, marginalisation is a result, not just of formal racism, but also of official policy. The State scheme for housing asylum-seekers in accommodation centres with reduced social welfare payments has been sharply criticised as discriminatory by the Irish Refugee Council and as possibly unconstitutional by the Free Legal Advice Centres (FLAC).[11] Under the system of direct provision, asylum-seekers are obliged to live in full-board accommodation centres around the State, including the former Mosney holiday camp in Co. Meath. Because people receive meals and laundry facilities, their weekly social welfare payments are accordingly reduced to €19.10 per adult and €9.60 per child. Groups working with asylum-seekers in direct provision have complained that it often leads to social exclusion, poverty, hopelessness and institutionalisation of residents. The Refugee Council pointed out that "As Ireland is a cash economy, asylum-seekers in direct provision are effectively obstructed from participating in almost all spheres of Irish society."[12] The system has also failed in its stated aim of deterring asylum applications. From a low of 39 asylum claims in Ireland in 1992, the numbers rose steadily during the 1990s. In 1999, 7,724 people made asylum claims, rising to 10,938 in 2000, 10,325 in 2001 and 11,634 in 2002.

PEOPLE WITH DISABILITIES

One of the lowlights of *The Irish Times'* survey of primary schools awaiting emergency repairs was Saint Safan's NS, Castlefin, Co. Donegal. The school was promised funding for health-and-safety refurbishments to provide a disabled toilet for a wheelchair user who has been in the school for four years. Any time the boy needs to go to the toilet his father has to come down to the school and bring him home. His plight says a great deal about the situation of people with disabilities in Ireland.

Coming into the boom years, Ireland had an appallingly low level of services for people with disabilities and their families. Between 2000 and 2002 an extra €244 million was channelled into new residential, day and respite services to begin to address the backlog of investment. These improvements in funding effectively ceased with the 2003 budget, however, even though the effects of decades of neglect were still very far from being reversed. Only €13.3 million in extra funding was provided, a figure that made actual cutbacks in services inevitable.

In general, disability spending has a low priority in Ireland. According to Eurostat, benefits relating to disability accounted for almost 14 per cent of total spending on social protection in Finland and Luxembourg and an average of 8.1 per cent in the EU. Norway spends 16.4 per cent of total social benefits on disability. In France, Ireland and Greece, on the other hand, this portion is less than 6 per cent.

This has consequences. In June 2003, while Ireland was hosting the Special Olympics, for example, the Health Research Board published its National Intellectual Disability Database, mapping the needs of, and provision for, the very people whom the Special Olympics celebrate. A close look at the figures, which are for 2001, suggests that, while the situation improved in the boom years, there are still many problems and at least one scandal.

The scandal is that Ireland had, in 2001, 677 people with intellectual disabilities accommodated in psychiatric hospitals. There is nothing to suggest that the vast majority of these people suffer from any mental illness or psychiatric condition. They are simply dumped in these hospitals because there is nowhere else for them to go.

Putting people who are not mentally ill into psychiatric hospitals is generally regarded as the mark of a barbaric regime. It was one of the grossest abuses of human rights in the old Soviet Union and one of the reasons China is still the object of international condemnation. Even though the practice is being slowly phased out in Ireland, the very fact that it continues at all is deeply shameful.

The database also shows that 10 per cent of Ireland's intellectually disabled persons – that's around 2,500 people – get no State services at all. Of these, 515 people are on waiting lists for day or residential services, which is bad enough, especially for the 170 or so people whose disability is moderate, severe or profound. Even more alarming, however, is that 2,265 people not only have no services at present, but "have no identified requirement for services within the five-year period 2002–2006".

The key word here is "identified". Some of these people have mild disabilities and may not need much State provision in the next three years. But it's clear that 743 people in this category are seriously intellectually disabled and yet are getting no services at all. It is especially disturbing that at least 53 children who have a moderate, severe or profound intellectual disability are neither currently availing of services nor on any waiting list.

Overall, of the 26,668 people with intellectual disabilities, 2,440 people are either without services or without a major element of the services they need; 677 are in psychiatric hospitals; and 10,182 people who are currently receiving services require alternative, additional or enhanced services within the next three years. So half of the intellectually disabled population is in urgent need of extra provision.

Almost two-thirds of all children and adults with intellectual disability live in a home setting with parents, siblings, relatives or foster parents. Just over one in four of the population with moderate, severe or profound intellectual disability aged 35 years and over continue to live with their families. Planning for the future care of these individuals and avoiding crisis situations when family carers can no longer provide care is recognised as being critical. Yet very many of the carers are already elderly, and many say they are afraid to die while their children's future is so uncertain.

In general, the State has been extremely reluctant to concede the principle that people with disabilities have rights and that provision must start with an objective assessment of each individual's needs. Behind the caring rhetoric, this has been made brutally clear. The official Commission on the Status of People with Disabilities report in 1996 recommended that "An assessment of needs should be made at the onset of disability, resulting in a Statement of Needs which identifies the full spectrum of services required by the person concerned from a range of agencies, as well as their financial need." In the ironically titled "Towards Equal Citizenship: Progress Report on the Implementation of the Recommendations of the Commission on the Status of People with Disabilities", four years later, the Government, and in particular the Minister for Finance, Charlie McCreevy, made no bones about its view of this dangerous pinko principle:

> The Department of Finance cannot accept these recommendations which imply the underpinning by law of access to and provision of services for people with disabilities as a right. This right, if given a statutory basis, would be prohibitively expensive for the Exchequer and could lead to requests from other persons seeking access to health and other services without regard to the eventual cost of providing these services.

Time and again, this cold, sharp pin has punctured the rhetoric of equal citizenship. In 1996, the Commission wrote that "The unique needs of the individual person must be the paramount consideration when decisions are being made concerning the appropriate provision of education for that person." In 2001, the Government successfully appealed a High Court ruling that Jamie Sinnott, a young autistic man, had a right to an appropriate education for so long as he required it. The then Minister for Education, Michael Woods, explained that the Government would honour the awards of compensation made to Jamie and his mother Kathryn, but only on "an *ex gratia* basis": a charitable gesture, not a right.

In 2002, the Government was forced to withdraw its draft Disability Bill after outraged protests from disability groups because the bill granted no statutory rights. In 2003, the Minister for Justice, Michael McDowell, suddenly reversed Ireland's long-standing policy of supporting a UN Convention on the Rights of People with Disabilities, deeply embarrassing the Department of Foreign Affairs which had been, along with Mexico, the main sponsor of the proposal. Happy to pat disabled people on the head and anxious to bask in international approval for the Special Olympics, the Government was willing to promise these citizens anything except real citizenship.

6

WHY ONLY THE LITTLE
PEOPLE PAY TAXES

She was the ultimate symbol of vulgar wealth, a sleek, 325-foot, shimmering-white luxury yacht proudly displaying the Onassis signature, the yellow funnel. The ship had begun life in 1943 as the Canadian naval frigate *Stormont*, a convoy escort. The Greek shipping magnate Aristotle Onassis purchased her in 1948 for just $34,000 and converted her during the early 1950s into the most sumptuous private yacht that the world had ever seen, at the then phenomenal cost of more than $4 million. He called her *Christina O*, after his daughter whose own tragic death would later symbolise the other side of wealth.

The rich and famous found the offer of a cruise on the *Christina O* hard to resist. Winston Churchill, Marilyn Monroe, Princess Grace, Frank Sinatra, Maria Callas and, of course, Jacqueline Kennedy-Onassis enjoyed all the facilities of a yacht the size of a three-storey New York brownstone mansion. Yet the vulgarity could not be hidden. "Ari's Bar", where Onassis presented the young John F. Kennedy to Sir Winston Churchill, who was a frequent guest throughout his retirement, had tiny models that displayed the development of ships and shipping throughout history. On the wall was a map showing the daily position of the Onassis fleet. The circular bar was adorned with footrests and handholds of ornately carved and polished whales' teeth collected by Onassis' whalers. But the barstools were covered with the foreskin of a whale, and Onassis thought it was the height of wit to point this out to any woman who sat on one.

The stools have now been re-covered in fine leather, after an extensive refurbishment of the yacht in 1998. The middle deck now houses a banquet-size, split-level, formal dining room that seats up to 40 guests. Its Baccarat wall lamps are original. The porcelain service is by Bernardaud of Limoges, the glasses are Waterford crystal by John Rocha and the silverware is by Ercuis and Saint Hilaire of Paris.

According to the on-line promotional blurb for paying guests, alongside the dining hall is a raised music room with a grand piano and a pair of conversation areas. It contains a collection of Maria Callas memorabilia, including the only gold record awarded to her. On the main deck there is a new gym and, for guests in need of a bit more pampering, there is a new massage room and beauty salon. Renzo Romagnoli created the new Sports Lounge, featuring Onassis' original sextant wall lamps and gaming tables with large, comfortable seating. New guest and service elevators were installed for efficient circulation onboard.

Spanning her massive stern is the open pool deck where opera diva Maria Callas loved to relax during her tumultuous relationship with Onassis. Its centrepiece is the bronze-bordered pool inlaid with mosaic frescos of ancient Crete. To the delight of guests, at the push of a button the bottom raises to the deck level, becoming an instant dance floor. The area has been freshened with glistening varnished handrails and treatments over rich teak decks.

Aft is the Lapis Lounge where Elizabeth Taylor and Richard Burton loved to relax in the sitting-room in front of the fireplace whose mantle was covered in deep-blue lapis lazuli. Its oak and iroko panelling is decorated with original works by Renoir, Le Corbusier and de Chirico. Forward on the same deck, past the central atrium and spiral staircase, the original guest staterooms, which Marilyn Monroe, Eva Peron, Greta Garbo and John Wayne once occupied, have been reconfigured. Each air-conditioned and soundproofed suite now has a large seating area, a bureau, a walk-in closet, twin or double beds and large portholes. The original bathing salons have been replaced with luxurious *en suite* marble bathrooms with showers. Each suite is equipped with a full entertainment system with TV, DVD and CD players. In addition, on the lower aft deck, eight elegant new staterooms have been fitted out, offering the same style and elegance as the original suites.

Forward of the atrium and concierge office, the original semicircular dining room, where Onassis once brokered blockbuster deals with J. Paul Getty, King Faud and the Saudi Royals, has been converted into an elegant library. The reception hall that hosted some of the 20th century's most famed wedding receptions – Princess Grace and Prince Rainier of Monaco in 1954 and Onassis' 1968 marriage to Jacqueline Kennedy – has been elegantly updated with sofas, armchairs, cocktail tables and accent pieces by Giorgetti. It also converts into a state-of-the-art cinema.

Outside and aft, the original boat deck has been converted into a spacious "Jacuzzi deck", complete with alfresco dining facilities, a large circular bar and a raised sun terrace with spa pool and teak *chaise-longues*. Farther aft, the plane deck, where Onassis kept his seaplane, is now a helipad.

Why is all of this of the slightest interest to Irish taxpayers? Because they paid for it. According to reports in May 2003, a consortium of wealthy Irish businessmen and professionals purchased the *Christina O* for $50 million. As early as October 2001, indeed, the *Sunday Business Post* had reported that

> a small but exclusive party was held aboard the boat the week before last. The guests included Michael Smurfit, Dermot Desmond, Michael Fingleton, chief executive of Irish Nationwide, and former Fianna Fáil fund-raiser Paul Kavanagh. Also present was leading tax lawyer Ivor Fitzpatrick, who advised former Taoiseach Charles Haughey on his tax litigation, and Greek businessmen who are also believed to be involved in the

> yacht deal. There are tax benefits in investing in
> shipping, according to one source, because capital
> cost can be offset against income.[1]

Irish tax law allows the purchasers of the *Christina O*, which is available for hire and is therefore regarded as a business, to claim capital allowances for this purchase and for the yacht's refurbishment and to set these costs against their Irish income for tax avoidance. This is estimated to have cost the Irish Exchequer €25 million. The Dáil was informed that the Revenue Commissioners were "fully aware" of the situation, although Minister of State for Finance Tom Parlon asserted that the Exchequer "must and will" protect taxpayers against such dubious activities which threaten to erode the tax base. Parlon also said, however, that he was unable to comment on the specifics of the case, citing confidentiality in individual and corporate taxpayer affairs.

All of this seems to be perfectly legal. Ireland also has, however, a stubborn culture of outright tax evasion. It survives not least because the perpetrators get away with it. Consider the dealings of some Irish citizens with the tax authorities in recent years.

THE PROPERTY DEVELOPER

The Property Developer had been in business at least since 1970, but he paid no tax at all until the 1988 tax amnesty, when he made a payment of €79,000 for the years between 1970/71 and 1988/89. This was a pittance and, even under the terms of the amnesty, the Revenue didn't think it was an adequate payment. But the tax authorities never got round to asking for a further payment.

During the 1990s, the developer and his family were involved in at least 35 active million-pound-plus property-development companies, including several major industrial estates, office blocks, apartment blocks, townhouse schemes and a shopping centre. His recent developments were valued at over €125 million.

Yet, in 2000, the Revenue wrote off €442,000 in Corporation Tax owed by one of this developer's companies since 1988. Its demand for the money was returned undelivered in 1990. The Revenue did nothing about it until 2000 when it decided to write off the money on the basis that neither of the directors of the company could be contacted. The company had failed to register its issued share capital, the names of its directors, a business address or any annual returns. The Revenue never made a connection between this company and the individual developer, his tax amnesty payment or his other companies.

Any co-ordinated look at this man's businesses, even a cursory glance, would have shown up glaring anomalies. He had 35 companies registered for Corporation Tax, 25 for VAT but none for PAYE/PRSI. While his core business was always property development, his tax cases were spread over various tax districts due to a wide variation of declared activities.

The Corporation Tax returns he did make were rarely filed for the proper periods. His companies were typically informally dissolved after the completion of a project, without a formal wind-up or final statement of affairs providing information on the sale of property or disposal of cash and other assets which would allow an assessment of tax liabilities.

The man's companies paid a total of just €0.25 million in Corporation Tax, but got VAT repayments from the Revenue of €6 million more than the companies had actually paid in VAT. One of the companies, which constructed two townhouse developments and an apartment block in the early 1990s and sold them for €10 million, was described at the time in its certified accounts in the company record office as dormant.

Putting the Revenue off the scent does not seem to have been too hard. In response to a returned demand for €34,000 VAT arrears arising from four tax audits, a Revenue field officer called to the registered address of one of the companies which had developed 36 houses to the value of €2.5 million without paying VAT or Corporation Tax. The official was told that the company had transferred to another address and that the whereabouts of the directors were unknown. At the second address, the official was informed that the company no longer existed. Yet both of the buildings the official called to were owned by the developer's company, a fact that could have been established with relative ease. The VAT arrears were written off.

This same developer was registered for Residential Property Tax (RPT). He sold his house for €3.9 million but the Revenue did not consider

him to have any RPT liability because his declared
income was below the income threshold.

THE TWO PUBLICANS

From the early 1990s Publican A has, through
various companies, been involved at different
stages in the operation of three pubs owned by
Publican B. Each of these newly formed companies registered for tax, obtained Tax Clearance
Certificates (TCCs) and renewed the pub licence.
Each then followed a behaviour pattern that
outsmarted and rendered useless the normal
Revenue procedures in this area.

The companies were partly tax compliant (for
VAT) during the first year of their operation. At
the end of the year an instalment arrangement for
paying off €1,000 per month was agreed with
Revenue for the VAT arrears, and the TCC was
issued enabling the publican to get the licence
renewed.

Once this was done the instalment arrangement was immediately abandoned and by the
third year the companies had large VAT arrears.
These were mainly estimated by the Revenue
because of the companies' failure to make returns.

At this point, the companies ceased to trade
and were dissolved. No annual returns were sent
to the Companies Registration Office. The pub
licence was transferred to the owner, Publican B,
who successfully obtained a TCC and a renewal of
the licence. Publican A's liabilities were written off
by the Revenue: €146,000 in one audit sample
taken by the Comptroller and Auditor General

and a total of €100,000 in two further cases relating to Publican A.

An interim period followed during which the business was totally non-compliant: in one case VAT returns were not filed for an unbroken three years. The dissolved company was then replaced by another with Publican A as a director and a "clean" tax record. The cycle starts all over again.

At the time of the Comptroller and Auditor General's report for 2001, Publican A's companies had not made any Corporation Tax returns. Publican B had declared only one of his ten directorships to Revenue; one of his companies acquired eight properties, mainly pubs and hotels, in the period 1987 to 1997 while deregistered for tax. On a licence-renewal application, three of the pubs declared annual turnover of between €1 million and €2.5 million.

In all, 22 companies which operated pubs owned by Publican B were dissolved without a formal wind-up or statement of affairs; no company returns were made to the Companies Registration Office during the period of incorporation.

THE LEISURE-SECTOR OPERATOR
He and his family had interests for over 12 years in 18 companies that ran 11 bars, nightclubs and hotels. Three of these companies were still active in 2002, while the others were dissolved or liquidated. Companies Registration Office registration or filing requirements were not fully met for any of the 18 companies.

All of these companies were partly or totally

non-compliant for taxes: some submitted tax returns but did not make payments; companies were registered for Corporation Tax but did not submit returns; a receiver of one of the companies generated and paid substantial amounts of tax while running a business which had made no returns while controlled by the original owner.

VAT audits of a number of the operator's companies identified underpayments and evasion. Each, however, was treated as a single case and not linked to the operator.

Yet the man's current nightclub business is run by a company that received a Tax Clearance Certificate even though it is not registered for VAT or PAYE. The previous owner was registered for these taxes, so the premises was on Revenue's records.

Excise licences have been issued to this operator up to one year after the date on which, in theory, the operator should not have been in business without a licence. Companies conducting some of the businesses did not have any excise licence but sheltered under a licence held by unrelated operators of other bars in a complex. Yet this same operator benefited from tax write-offs of €690,000.

THE PHOENIX

One of the most important safeguards against this kind of tax fraud is the issuing of Tax Clearance Certificates. TCCs are required for many areas of business: getting public-sector contracts, obtaining various licences and getting State grants. Yet the

Comptroller and Auditor General's audit found the following.

- Companies had obtained TCCs without registering for any tax head.
- Companies obtained TCCs by registering for one tax, for example Corporation Tax, but not for the taxes which would give rise to their main tax liabilities – VAT and PAYE. In many instances, pubs had obtained TCCs without registering for those taxes.
- Persistent tax dodgers subverted the regulations and obtained TCCs simply by changing the name of the business and/or establishing another company. The tax histories of the company owners were not considered in the vetting of applications for tax clearance.
- TCCs were issued to companies that had serious tax arrears merely on foot of a pledge or an arrangement to pay off arrears, leaving Revenue at a loss when the arrangement collapsed.
- One "phoenix" company with over 60 employees filed a "nil" return for PAYE but received a TCC.[2]

At the end of 2002 there were 26 cases of serious tax fraud at various stages of investigation or prosecution. Just three of these were before the Courts in 2002, while the Director of Public Prosecutions had given directions to prosecute in another four. During the year a grand total of three convictions were secured in the Courts, and even in these cases the punishments imposed were puny.

- In October 2002, a cattle dealer/haulier was convicted of failure to make returns of income for five years, giving rise to "substantial" evasion of tax. He received a fine of €3,000.
- In November 2002, a company director was convicted of making fraudulent VAT repayment claims. He was given custodial sentences of three months on each of two charges, both of which were suspended on condition that he repaid to Revenue the tax defrauded.
- In December 2002, a builder was convicted for making a false income tax and VAT return. He was fined €2,540.

In all, then, tax fraud in 2002 was punished with a grand total of €5,540 in fines and no prison sentences were actually served. The contrast with the attitude to social welfare fraud is striking. A total of 245 cases were forwarded to the Chief State Solicitor's office. Some 167 cases were finalised in court – in which five offenders were served with prison sentences, 28 received suspended sentences, 78 were fined, a total of 32 received the Probation Act and the remainder were struck out, dismissed or bound to the peace.

In 2002, Revenue audited 16,186 cases and the audits yielded €286.83 million. Over the same period, the Department of Social and Family Affairs carried out a total of 341,000 reviews of social welfare claims and realised savings of €282.7million.[3] In other words, for roughly the same amount of money saved or earned for the Exchequer, social welfare claimants were subjected to over 20 times more scrutiny than taxpayers.

Nor is there much evidence that the general attitude to tax evasion had changed greatly in 2003, in spite of the stream of revelations about offshore accounts. In June, a prominent midlands businessman, Brendan Galligan of Mullingar Travel, was convicted in Mullingar, Co. Westmeath on two counts of tax evasion. He was one of more than 400 investors in an unauthorised investment scheme sold by National Irish Bank. He failed to disclose income he had used to invest in the NIB scheme and also further sums invested at the Bank of Ireland and Woodchester Credit Lyonnais. The amount of money in these accounts was not disclosed, but the scale of the sums involved can be gauged by the fact that he had made a payment of IR£185,000 in respect of the two years alluded to and followed that with a €400,000 payment in the days leading up to his court appearance.

He was convicted of knowingly or wilfully delivering incorrect income tax returns to the Inspector of Taxes in respect of the years 1992–93 and 1993–94. The judge imposed fines totalling €1,500 in respect of the two offences – hardly a huge sum for a man with assets of this order.

In some respects, it is surprising that wealthy

individuals in Ireland resort to outright tax evasion at all. The yield from wealth taxes is not only very low, but it is actually falling. The amount of Capital Acquisitions Tax (which comprises Inheritance, Gift, Discretionary Trust and Probate Taxes) paid in 2002 was €151 million, over 10 per cent below the 2001 yield of €168 million. The yield of €619 million from Capital Gains Tax in 2002 was €139 million below the budget estimate and €257 million less than the 2001 yield – a drop of almost 30 per cent. From a total tax yield of almost €40 billion, these two areas of taxation thus contributed just €770 million: less than a fiftieth of the total.

There is, moreover, ample scope for legal tax avoidance as opposed to illegal tax evasion. A study, compiled by the Revenue Commissioners statistics division and published with the 2003 budget, found that 18 per cent of the 400 top earners in 1999/2000 were paying tax at less than 15 per cent.[4] Just over one-tenth were paying between 15 and 30 per cent, while 71 per cent were taxed at between 30 and 46 per cent. About 12 per cent were paying less than 5 per cent tax. This was at a time when the lower rate of tax for most PAYE workers was 26 per cent, rising to 44 per cent as soon as a single worker earned more than IR£17,000. We thus had a situation in which a poorly paid worker was paying tax at 44 per cent, while a very wealthy individual could be paying as little as 5 per cent.

Of the 117 wealthy individuals studied by the Revenue who had effective tax rates of less than 30 per cent, 29 paid no tax at all; 22 paid at less than

5 per cent; 12 paid between 5 and 9 per cent; 10 paid between 10 and 14 per cent; 12 paid between 15 and 19 per cent; 19 paid between 20 and 24 per cent; and 13 paid between 25 and 30 per cent. Most of these individuals were therefore getting away with paying less than 15 per cent tax.

They were able to do this by availing of tax reliefs and loopholes. The total annual cost of tax allowances and reliefs to the Exchequer is in the region of €8.5 billion. The significance of this figure is obvious when compared with total tax and excise revenue of around €40 billion. Much of this is made up of reliefs to industry and business, which arguably have social and economic advantages that make them worthwhile, but significant amounts are lost through schemes whose worth to society is highly dubious.

The main tax shelters identified in the Revenue report as creating the extraordinarily low effective rates of the wealthy individuals they studied are the property-based capital allowance incentives. They put the tax losses involved as follows:

- multi-storey car-parks (€9,725,723)
- hotels (€12,095,933)
- miscellaneous property-based capital allowances (€46,421,412)

The other tax shelters – heritage homes (€4,105,355), loan interest (€846,863), film relief (€152,368) and miscellaneous reliefs (€939,606) – generated much lower but still significant losses.

It is impossible to calculate with precision the sum total of Revenue losses through these schemes, however, because, astonishingly, only some of them require the recipients to make a return of the exempt income to the Revenue Commissioners. Public spending is subject to detailed scrutiny and audit. The Department of Finance's Public Expenditure Division evaluates spending plans and maintains tight control. The Comptroller and Auditor General examines where the money has gone and whether it gave value for money. The Dáil's Public Accounts Committee asks the heads of Government departments and agencies to account for their spending.

But there are no corresponding checks on tax breaks – who gets them, how much they cost, whether they are value for money.

The 2003 Finance Bill, for example, was the first to provide for beneficiaries of three of these tax provisions – namely, stallion fees, forestry and greyhound-stud fees – to declare the income generated by these businesses. The horse-breeding industry was exempted from paying tax on stud fees 30 years ago. Yet top stallions such as last year's horse of the year Rock of Gibraltar, part-owned by Sir Alex Ferguson, can earn stud fees of €10 million a year. No tax at all is paid on this income.

The cost of an extraordinary range of tax exemptions is classified by the Revenue as "not quantifiable".

- Certain payments made by a person carrying on a trade or profession to an Irish university or other qualifying educational establishment.

- Relief for donations made to certain bodies engaged in the promotion of the arts.
- Exemption in respect of certain income derived from the leasing of farmland.
- Expenditure on certain buildings in designated inner city areas.
- Relief for new shares purchased on issue by employees.
- Relief for donations made to Cospoir (the National Sports Council).
- Relief for investment in research and development.
- Exemption in respect of stallion stud fees.
- Exemption of profits arising from commercially managed woodlands.
- Relief from averaging of farm profits.
- Exemption for income arising from payments in respect of personal injuries.
- Exemption of certain payments made by Haemophilia HIV Trust.
- Exemption in respect of income arising from certain patents.
- Exemption in respect of payments made under the Enterprise Allowance Scheme.
- Exemption of income from foreign trusts.
- Exemption of lump-sum retirement payments.
- Relief for allowable motor expenses.
- Tapering relief allowable for taxation of car benefits-in-kind.
- Relief for gifts to The Enterprise Trust Ltd.
- Reduced tax rate of 10 per cent for authorised unit trust schemes.

- Reduced tax rate of 10 per cent for special investment schemes.
- Exemption of certain grants made by Údarás na Gaeltachta.
- Relief for donations made by companies to First Step Ltd.
- Reliefs for activities related to the Customs House Docks Area and Shannon Airport Customs-Free zone.
- Relief for investment income reserved for policy holders in life-assurance companies.
- Allowances for double-rent, owner-occupier and expenditure on historic buildings in Urban Renewal areas.
- Relief for various business-related expenses such as staff recruitment, rent, legal fees and other general expenses.
- Exemption in certain circumstances on quoted bearer Eurobonds.
- Exemption of payments made as compensation for loss of office.
- Renewal scheme for traditional seaside resorts.
- Donations to third-level institutions.
- Exemption of scholarship income.
- Donations to Public Libraries.

Even those tax breaks that are quantified may have hidden costs. The tax breaks for multi-storey car-parks have no obvious social benefit, and in some cases actually cost the public money over and above the cost of the tax foregone. The Comptroller and Auditor General, for example,

published a report on the multi-storey car-park at
Beaumont Hospital in Dublin, built in 1998. This
facility created just 230 new parking spaces, at a
cost of €8.6 million. The work was done by
Howard Holdings PLC, a British property company, which in return gets most of the revenue
from parking fees until 2011. The developer also
got substantial tax breaks, which allowed him to
write off much of his costs. According to the
Comptroller and Auditor General, this ended up
costing the public between €9 million and €13
million more than if the car-park simply had been
built as a public project.

The way in which these tax breaks become law
is often extraordinary. A last-minute Finance Bill
change in 1994, section 19, gave retrospective tax
relief in relation to leased art works in stately
homes, which benefited just one taxpayer, Ken
Rohan, and let him off a large pending tax bill.

Even in the 2003 budget, when great play was
made of the Government's determination to close
down tax shelters, a new one was introduced with
no accountability or scrutiny. Just as the 2003
Finance Bill, which gives effect to the budget, was
being wrapped up in the Dáil, the Minister for
Finance, Charlie McCreevy, introduced a sudden
amendment giving new tax breaks to private hospital developers. As he explained, it was "devised
as a result of a meeting I held last November with
certain constituents". While McCreevy had been
insisting that public health spending be subjected
to the closest scrutiny, this measure got none at all.

The Minister read the text of the amendment to

the Dáil and very roughly outlined its origins, though without giving any indication of the cost to the Exchequer. The entire debate then went as follows:

Ms Burton: Who are the promoters?

Mr R. Bruton: I wish to speak ...

Ms Burton: I indicated first. Who are the promoters and who did the Department meet on February 24th? Who were the representations from and to what kind of hospital facility is the Minister referring?

Mr R. Bruton: Why is the Minister including passive investors in this concession?

Mr McCreevy: I am not.

Mr R. Bruton: The Minister said he was.

Mr McCreevy: I am including the existing schemes, subject to the overall limit of €25,000.

Mr Rabbitte: Who is this doctor we heard about?

Mr McCreevy: He is a doctor in my constituency. He is an ordinary GP situated in the Naas area whose name was given to Deputy Stagg. He may even be a supporter of the deputy.

Mr Ó Caoláin: I object to the wording of the question that is being put, that the Bill is hereby passed. We oppose passage of the Bill and ask the Chair to correct the declaration that the Bill is now being passed. That is not the case.

Acting Chairman: As it is now 1.30 p.m. I am required to put the following question in accordance with an order of the Dáil of this day: "That the amendments set down by the Minister for Finance and not disposed of are hereby made to the Bill, Report Stage is hereby completed and the Bill is hereby passed."

And that was the full extent of the public scrutiny of the kind of health spending that Charlie McCreevy wishes to encourage. The cost to the public purse is at least €9 million and could rise to €63 million depending on the number of private hospitals built.

The scale of tax reliefs on personal pensions is also worth noting. In 1999, the last year for which we have figures, twice as much public money went on tax relief for pension saving than on social welfare pensions. Tax relief on pension saving cost €1,100 million and exemption of pension-fund income from tax cost €1,300 million, compared to €1,140 million on social welfare pensions. Tax relief on pension contributions is also skewed towards the well-off because the lower paid get tax relief at 20 per cent while top earners get tax relief at 42 per cent. Many wealthy individuals take advantage of this to exempt up to 30 per cent of their income from tax by investing it in their pension.

Even leaving aside these tax shelters, there are good reasons to believe that a great deal of income in Ireland still escapes the tax net. In the Revenue's Statistical Bulletin dealing with the latest year for which there are full figures, 1999–2000, there were just 70,874 people declaring incomes of between €35,000 and €40,000; 88,411 between €40,000 and €50,000; 47,489 between €50,000 and €60,000; 37,027 between €60,000 and €75,000; 23,340 between €75,000 and €100,000; 12,580 between €100,000 and €150,000; and 9,891 earning over €150,000.

These figures, it is important to remember, include many married couples with two incomes being assessed jointly for tax purposes. Which is why hardly anyone actually believes them. They make no sense at all. In April 1999, for example, 15 houses in a new development in Carrickmines in Dublin, costing about IR£1 million each, were sold within four hours of going on the market. In that year, some 55 million credit-card transactions, worth IR£3.3 billion, were transacted. Around 30,000 people took ski holidays that winter, in addition to the 700,000 who had taken summer sun holidays by the end of October.

Put the Revenue figures beside new car sales in 1999 and 2000 and you get some idea of their credibility. According to the Revenue figures, about 380,000 Irish individuals or couples earned more than €30,000. Yet about 295,000 people registered a new car in these years. Unless we assume that a huge proportion of those who could possibly be able to afford a new car went out and bought one, the income figures seem incredible.

Look at it another way. According to the Central Statistics Office's Household Budget Survey for 1999-2000, almost a quarter of Irish households had two or more cars. That translates into about 300,000 taxpayers. Since being able to afford to run two cars is a reasonable indication of a high income, there ought to be far more high earners than appear on the Revenue figures. This is especially obvious at the top end. By my calculations, in the years covered by the Revenue figures, 13,749 people in the Republic bought either a new BMW or a new Mercedes. (Many other luxury cars were sold as well, of course.)

This alone suggests that the figure of 22,471 people earning over €100,000 is deeply suspect. No one outside of that income bracket could possibly afford one of these cars. Unless we assume that well over half of these people bought a Mercedes or a BMW in that particular year, the figure just doesn't convince. Another way to look at this is to take a few of the professions whose earnings we know about.

In January 2000, for example, prison officers were earning an average of €929 a week or, on an annualised basis, over €48,000 a year. Members of the Garda Síochána were earning an average of €875 a week at the same time – €45,500 on an annualised basis.

There were 3,200 prison officers and 11,700 gardaí – a total of 14,900. Yet in total there are supposedly only 88,411 people with incomes in the €40,000–50,000 bracket. Is it really likely that a sixth of this total could be accounted for by just two public service jobs?

In 1999 the average earnings of primary and secondary teachers were €35,000. Two teachers married to each other and taxed jointly would thus have a before-tax income of €70,000. There were 40,000 primary and secondary teachers, but only 37,027 people in total with incomes supposedly in the €60,000–€75,000 income bracket. Even if we assume that all the teachers were taxed as single people, they make up an incredible proportion of the 90,000 people on incomes of between €30,000 and €35,000.

Or take an example from the high end of the scale. We know that in the year 2001 the insurance industry paid out fees of €440 million to lawyers involved in compensation cases. Even if every one of the 6,500 lawyers in the country was getting an equal share of this money, that would work out at about €70,000 each from this source of income alone.

If the figures are to be believed, the number of people earning over €100,000 more than doubled between 2000 and 2002. The 22,471 people declaring incomes of over €100,000 in 2000 rose to 53,500 in 2002.[5] That this should have happened in a period when the economy was slowing down is simply incredible. It is far more likely that a greater number of wealthy taxpayers decided to declare more of their income, perhaps because they were confident of being able to get tax relief on much of it.

The obvious conclusion is that very many taxpayers understate their incomes by a significant amount. And since this option is not open to those who pay PAYE, the strong likelihood is that these people are to be found in the self-employed and farming sectors and among people who have significant earnings from sources other than employment. This suspicion is borne out by the most recent figures, which continue to show extremely low tax returns from these sectors.

In 2002, 110,000 farmers paid an estimated €126 million income tax – an average of just €1,145 each. Even allowing for those on low incomes who are outside the tax net, this is an extraordinarily low figure. At the same time, 235,000 self-employed people (including farmers) earned almost €10 billion and paid just €1.9 billion in tax, an effective tax rate of less than 20 per cent. Of the

53,500 people earning more than €100,000, almost 17,000 were self-employed and they earned an average of €224,000. Yet they paid on average just €50,000 in tax – an effective tax rate of 22 per cent.

All of this doesn't just mean that taxes are not spread fairly. It also affects the equity of public provision, especially higher education. Higher-education grants are means-tested. A would-be student whose parents are PAYE workers is assessed for eligibility on the basis of the family's actual income. But the children of self-employed people and farmers are often assessed on a declared income that may be much lower than the reality and that takes no account of assets. The 1993 de Buitleir report into third-level student support cited a case where one prospective student's father had net assets of over IR£500,000 but his reckonable income for grants purposes was just over IR£6,000 – with the result that the applicant qualified for a full grant. One farmer had 122 acres and net assets of IR£215,000, but his annual income for grant purposes was only IR£15,000.

Nothing has changed in the decade since the report was published. According to a recent Dáil answer, farmers received more than 1,000 of the 6,000 grants given by 26 local authorities in 2002. Nearly 400 self-employed people received grants, but only 137 from homes headed by unskilled manual workers did so.

What all of this means is that it is possible to raise taxes in Ireland without imposing punitive rates of taxation on the vast majority of ordinary workers. At the moment, the majority of compliant taxpayers deeply resents taxation because it feels, with some justification, that many better-off people are getting away without paying their share. A fair and efficient system, backed up by serious penalties for evasion, would both raise more income for social investment and make the majority of compliant taxpayers feel more open to a genuine debate about what they want from their society and how much they should pay for it.

7

SELLING OFF THE FAMILY SILVER

There are some things that the free market, left to
itself, does very well. It is extremely good at
creating, marketing and distributing consumer
products. In a developed society, it is by far the
best way to turn technological innovations into
saleable commodities. For the vast bulk of
products that consumers can choose to buy or not
to buy, the market works.

From the late 1970s onwards, however, the idea
has taken hold that the free market is also the best
way to provide the things that most of us have
little choice about buying: water, electricity, public
transport and so on. The basic claims of the neo-
liberal economists who have influenced public
policy around the world are that even in these
areas of public provision the private sector would
be more efficient; private companies would be
better able to finance the large investments
needed; and privatisation would create

competition, bringing down prices and improving the service to the consumer.

Ireland has been relatively slow to privatise State-owned enterprises, and it is worth noting that the Irish boom occurred in an economy that had, up to the late 1990s, largely bucked the trend of privatisation. In recent years, however, the privatisation programme has been accelerated. The State has sold off public companies such as Eircom, Irish Sugar, Irish Life, the Agricultural Credit Corporation, Cablelink and others. The Irish Exchequer has accrued revenues of over €8.2 billion (9 per cent of GNP for 2001) from these sales. (The direct cost of the privatisation process, however, has so far amounted to €2.2 billion or 27 per cent of the proceeds.) The Government has made it clear, moreover, that it intends to carry on this process, with the public transport companies (Aer Rianta, CIE, Dublin Bus, Aer Lingus) and the Electricity Supply Board as the most prominent items on the agenda.

The obvious question, then, is whether the privatisation of public utilities actually works. Are privatised utilities more efficient? Do they invest more money? Do they provide a better and cheaper service? Obvious as they may seem, these questions have not been asked with any great persistence by the advocates of privatisation. The greater efficiency of the private sector is an article of faith, and true believers don't really need to look at the evidence. Especially when the evidence is as damning as it appears to be in the countries that have sold off public utilities with the greatest gusto.

NEW ZEALAND

No country privatised as quickly or as thoroughly as New Zealand did in the 1980s. And none has been more thoroughly chastened by the experience. The New Zealand experience, and the lessons learned from it, are best outlined by the country's Deputy Prime Minister, Jim Anderton, in a speech to the Commonwealth Business Forum on May 10th 2002.

It is difficult to outline New Zealand's recent experience of private-public partnerships without considering the chaos that economic policy can wreak. In the mid-eighties, the New Zealand Government of the day began a programme of privatisation. It was continued by successive Governments through to the election of the present Labour-Alliance Coalition in 1999. In that time almost every configuration of public and private ownership has been tried.

For many years, the term "public-private partnership" was a code word for privatisation. In New Zealand today, partnership in almost every strategic sector is emerging because of a need for the public sector to re-enter the frame. As far as I am aware, no other country in the eighties and nineties deregulated and privatised as far or as fast as New Zealand attempted ...

Attempts to create a market in the electricity industry led, in 1998, to blackouts lasting several weeks in our largest city, Auckland. The industry was privatised first by handing out tradable share certificates to customers of local, community-owned retail companies ... Individual share-holdings were quickly aggregated into privately-owned monopolies. Consumers were encouraged to change electricity suppliers, and then found it almost impossible to do so. Energy companies couldn't put together switching agreements that ensured electricity stayed connected, meters were read and customers received bills. As recently as this year, a national drive to reduce energy consumption by ten per cent had to be launched at the height of winter. The market failed to anticipate demand and ensure adequate supply to meet it ... No one now seriously expects the electricity market to deliver adequately in the foreseeable future.

In telecommunications, privatisation brought net disinvestment in technology for most of the nineties. A near monopoly firm was able to increase consumer prices every year, even when the availability of new technology should have been driving prices down. International comparisons revealed New Zealanders paying very high sums for line rentals, domestic and international toll calls and mobile services ... Poor competitive conditions produced poor investment decisions and unsatisfactory consumer service.

More seriously, the prospect of non-metropolitan areas falling steadily behind in the availability of broadband services threatens the viability of entire regions. The Government has responded by introducing industry specific regulations. The Government is also again entering the telecommunications sector, albeit in a minor way. We are piloting broadband schemes in partnership with local communities and telecommunications companies aimed at ensuring all of New Zealand can harness a digital future.

In the mid-eighties, the public sector owned four commercial banks. By the early nineties, it owned none, and not a single major financial institution was New Zealand owned. Many parts of

New Zealand lost banking services altogether. Resentment at the level of bank charges rose every year, as banks repatriated very high levels of profits overseas. The absence of any significant New Zealand-owned financial institutions brought widespread further problems. The flow of profits out of New Zealand seriously worsened our current account deficit, at a time when it was already critically impaired. The loss of services from regional New Zealand undermined the viability of those regions. As banks left, so too other businesses would depart. The new Government has responded by allowing the publicly-owned New Zealand Post to establish a "People's Bank."

In 1993 the Government of the day sold New Zealand Rail. Its purchasers this year announced an intention to withdraw from passenger rail services altogether. Rail services in many parts of the country are under threat. The Government has exchanged letters with Tranz Rail on a possible agreement to re-purchase the Auckland rail corridor. In some parts of the country – such as the lower half of the South Island – central government is offering to subsidise services directly, in partnership with local government.

Supporters of the market usually held out Air New Zealand as a model of privatisation. In 1988 Air New Zealand was sold to a consortium for $660 million. The Government of the day retained what was called a "kiwi share". It ensured a majority of New Zealand directors on the board. The structure was designed to secure New Zealand's bilateral landing rights. As many of you will know, this glittering jewel in the Crown of the market has fallen on hard times. It purchased the major Australian airline Ansett last year at too high a price. In September, Air New Zealand was forced to write off its purchase of Ansett, with a loss of $1.3 billion. These circumstances have left the Government with little alternative but to take an active interest in the future viability of an Air New Zealand, for the wider good of the country.

Airlines, like railways, roads, telecommunications and financial architecture are part of the cement that enables the market to function. They have to be there when you want to use them. One of the theoretical strengths of the market is its ability to clear away inefficient firms and replace them with more efficient investment. But New Zealand's experience has been that failure of an infrastructural business has knocked over many efficient businesses. The Auckland power blackouts, for example, wiped out many small businesses, and significantly dented GDP. The growth lost through an episode like that is never recovered ...

The lessons of running a successful public enterprise have been demonstrated by our Post Office. NZ Post offers the cheapest standard letter rate in the world. It is highly profitable, it has a clear strategic focus, strong management, good disciplines, and a forward strategy including moving into banking and expanding overseas. The lesson is that public sector is not just public – it also has to be enterprising. The public sector cannot be successful where it attempts merely to stand still and administer. It needs to be accountable, innovative and adaptable. It needs to make good investment decisions, have clear objectives and it needs to meet the market.

In the case of the public sector, "meeting the market" means meeting the needs of the wider public who own it. The New Zealand experiment saw the public sector attempt to withdraw from investment in infrastructure. The experiment largely failed. Circumstance is bringing back the concept of public enterprise.

THE GREAT RAILWAY DISASTER

The decision to privatise the railway system in Britain was part of a far-reaching programme of privatisation between 1979 and 1997, during which State assets were sold for UK£65 billion and more than a million workers were transferred from the public to the private sector. Selling off British Rail, however, was to be the most symbolic statement of Margaret Thatcher's ideology. It would show that many public utilities and infrastructure services, which were earlier thought to be "natural monopolies", could in fact be privatised and subjected to competition through market forces.

British Rail was sold by John Major's Tory Government in 1996, for a total of UK£5 billion, after it had been broken up into a number of different entities that were to operate in competition with each other. The plan was that passenger trains would be run by 25 Train Operating Companies on franchises; the trains would be owned by three Rolling Stock Companies and the railway signalling, tracks, bridges, stations and other stock infrastructure by a company that would be known as Railtrack. Railtrack was sold for UK£1.93 billion in a public flotation in 1996.

For the first four years, Railtrack made a profit. Its share prices rose steeply and the shares paid growing dividends. Much of the profit came from rent and sale of property that the company had so cheaply acquired. But the main source of income was the track-access charges paid by the train operators. These charges were fixed by the Government-appointed Rail Regulator, who was also responsible for monitoring efficiency and safety inside Railtrack.

The need to increase profit, however, meant reducing expenditure on maintenance, repair and related activities. Repair work was farmed out by Railtrack to contracting firms, all of whom competed with each other to minimise costs. This in turn had effects not only in terms of delays and congestion because of the poor condition of some tracks, but also in terms of the safety of travel and increased accident rates. Investigations into the fatal Hatfield train crash on October 17th 2000, which brought Britain's rail system to a halt, and into two other rail accidents (Southhall in 1997 and Ladbroke Grove in 1999) have revealed that the number of maintenance workers had fallen by over 60,000 from 159,000 in 1992, even though the number of trains had increased.

Such accidents and delays were not just bad for passengers. They were also expensive for Railtrack – Hatfield alone is estimated to have cost Railtrack UK£1 billion in compensation. In addition, for the benefit of passengers, the Rail Regulator set targets for punctuality. As aggressively competing railway companies increased the number of trains, this meant more traffic congestion and more delays. Railtrack was fined

by the Rail Regulator for every delay judged to be
its fault (that is, resulting from track repair work
or emergency speed restrictions because of poor
track conditions). In 2000, this meant a fine of
UK£10 million. Railtrack also had to compensate
train operators for each delayed train.

These unforeseen expenses substantially
increased Railtrack's costs, even while they were
part of a privatised system that was providing
deteriorating services, in terms of reduced lines on
non-profitable routes, more delays on almost all
routes and worse safety performance. After the
Hatfield crash, and with slower aggregate economic growth, private investment in the railway
system collapsed. This called into question the
Blair Government's much-touted "public-private
partnership" in the new Transport Policy, which
had envisaged the private sector contributing 70
per cent of the anticipated investment of UK£50
billion.

Railtrack's accumulated losses made it
impossible for it to service its growing debt.
Finally, in October 2001, when the Blair Government decided it would no longer release public
money to keep Railtrack afloat, the company was
forced into administration. The Transport Secretary, Stephen Byers, announced the Government's
intention to set up a not-for-profit company
limited under guarantee (Network Rail) to run the
rail network thereafter. This amounts to an
effective re-nationalisation of the rail transport
system, at least of the track and station network.
But the entire process is likely to turn out to be a

massively expensive waste of public funds. It would have been a far more efficient use of resources to have avoided this costly experiment altogether, and instead spent the money as direct public investment to improve the publicly owned services of the former British Rail. Before privatisation, public subsidies to British Rail in 1989–1990 were UK£885 million (in real prices). Total State support to the privatised rail industry is expected to hit UK£3.8 billion in 2003–2004. Ticket prices are among the most expensive in the world. Average rail prices in the UK in 1999 were around 30p per mile. In Italy the journey from Milan to Rome on 140 m.p.h. tilting trains cost just UK£36, or 9p a mile. The rate per mile between Madrid and Barcelona was just 10p. In 2001 a standard open return fare between London and Manchester cost UK£150 – a rise of 50 per cent in less than two years.

ELECTRICITY IN ENGLAND

At first glance, the privatisation of electricity provision in England looks like a great success. The service remained reliable and prices to small consumers have fallen in real terms by about 25 per cent since privatisation in 1990. In fact, however, these price reductions were paid for by taxpayers because assets owned by taxpayers were sold for only a fraction of their real value. Closer examination of the reasons for the reduction in prices suggests that the main reasons were not improvements in efficiency caused by the operation of markets The main factors were:

145

reductions of 30–40 per cent in fossil fuel prices; temporary price reductions due to the effective write-off of much of the pre-privatisation asset base; and a shift in the liabilities of the disastrously expensive and inefficient nuclear power generating industry off the balance sheets of the industry. Moreover, the price reductions will probably be temporary as prices will have to rise as old assets are replaced by new assets paid for at the full market price. This trend is becoming apparent in the transmission sector and for the period 2001–05 prices are predicted to fall by little more than 1 per cent per year. In any event, the 25 per cent inflation-adjusted drop in UK electricity prices over 15 years should be compared with the larger 36 per cent drop over 15 years in what was an almost entirely regulated US electricity market.

Competition, moreover, is diminishing. The initial 14 companies have been reduced to 6 dominant players, each of which has an effective monopoly in its own region. In fact the electricity industry throughout Europe has been concentrated into the hands of just a few companies. Three strong companies already look set to dominate Europe: EDF of France and EON and RWE of Germany. These companies already own three out of six of the dominant integrated generation/retail supply companies in Britain. An additional small number of regional companies, for example Endesa in Southern Europe and Vattenfall in Northern Europe, are thought likely to gain a strong position. The probable result is that electricity markets in Britain and the rest of Europe will be dominated by three or four international companies with little incentive to compete hard against each other.[1]

THE GREAT CALIFORNIA BLACKOUT

The deregulation of electricity in the United States has the great merit of having a series of un-equivocal outcomes.

- Reliability has decreased and blackouts have increased.
- Prices are both higher and more volatile.
- Low-income customers are at greater risk of being unable to afford to retain electricity service.
- There is a growing gap between the prices paid for electricity by large and small customers.
- Jobs have been lost both within the electricity industry and among industries that use electricity.
- There are new consumer problems, such as slamming, invasions of privacy and lack of information about consumer choices.

As a result, states that have adopted retail competition policies are reconsidering them and states that have not adopted such policies are reaffirming their determination. At least three states – California, Nevada and Oklahoma – have repealed their retail competition schemes. While almost half the states (24 states and the District of

Columbia) have adopted policies to promote retail electricity competition, 7 of the 24 have already postponed or abandoned competition, and more than half the states (26) have considered adopting competition and declined to do so.

What happened was that, once the owners of power stations got unregulated monopoly power, they started to turn the power on and off, deliberately creating scarcity. This, as was intended, drove the price very high. Turning generators on and off also created a great deal of wear and tear on plants and actually created physical scarcity because plants needed maintenance much more often. There were many more blackouts – 50 per cent more in California under deregulation than before. And these in turn also contributed to price rises, as companies desperately sought to buy electricity on the open market.

Electricity traders, such as the notorious Enron, came into the marketplace to take advantage of the situation. They figured out that when there is volatility in the supply, there is an opportunity to buy low and sell high. So the volatility that traders helped to create in California made enormous profits for them; trading profits doubled and tripled.

In California, wholesale electricity prices that were as low as 2.1 cents per kilowatt hour (kWh) in February 1999 shot up to 31.7 cents per kWh in December 2000. Blackouts rolled across the state. Manufacturing plants closed all over the west, putting their employees out of work. Massachusetts retail default price increases wiped out the 15 per cent rate cut provided by statute as New England wholesale prices almost tripled. In New York City, Consolidated Edison residential customers suffered a 43 per cent rate increase in June 2001. Until the World Trade Center catastrophe wiped out so much demand that New York City now has a supply surplus, experts were predicting that summer wholesale prices would rise another 46 per cent by 2005. Wholesale prices since 1997 have more than doubled in Chicago, the Upper Midwest, New York and New England; almost tripled in some parts of the South and more than tripled in other parts; and quadrupled in Texas.[2]

WATER FOR SALE

The Thatcher Government in the UK originally proposed to privatise the provision of water in 1984, but there was a very strong public campaign against the proposals and they were abandoned before the issue could influence the 1987 election. Once this was won, the privatisation plan was resurrected and implemented rapidly.

Privatisation did not create any competition. The companies were given monopolies in their regions for 25 years, without having to compete even once for the business.

The Government wrote off all the debts of the water companies before privatisation, worth over UK£5 billion. In addition, it gave the companies a "green dowry" of UK£1.6 billion to help them meet their environmental obligations. The Government also offered the companies for sale at a substantial discount, which has been assessed as equal to 22 per cent of their market value, measured as the difference between the issue price of the water companies' shares and the share price after the first week of trading.

The initial price regime, set as a political act before the regulator was established, was also extremely generous to the companies. As a result the pre-tax profits of the ten sewerage and water companies rose by 147 per cent between 1990/91 and 1997/98. The companies were given special exemption from paying Corporation Taxes on these profits. In a seven-year period the real value of the top director's pay increased by between 50 per cent and 200 per cent in most of the water companies.

These profits, though, came at public expense. Sewerage and water prices rose in real terms, adjusted for inflation, respectively by 42 per cent and 36 per cent. Even the rabidly pro-Conservative *Daily Mail* began to write about "The Great Water Robbery" in 1994, calling water privatisation "the biggest rip-off in Britain".

Nor did privatisation do anything for either investment or jobs. A House of Commons committee report in November 2000 pointed out that:

> For the period 1993–1998 water mains in poor condition (grades 4 and 5) increased from 9% to 11%, equating to £0.78bn worth of pipes moving into these categories. As of March 1998 (the latest assessments) 10% of critical sewers were also in a poor condition.[3]

Meanwhile employment in the water industry fell by 21.5 per cent, or 8,599, between 1990 and 2000.[4]

THE BUS TO NOWHERE

Even the World Bank, which has pushed privatisation programmes in many parts of the world,
acknowledges that the policy just doesn't live up
to the claims made for it. A 1999 World Bank
report *Buses in Great Britain: Privatisation, Deregulation and Competition* makes grim reading for
those who see private ownership as a solution to
public transport problems.

Reductions in the levels of public subsidy after
privatisation in the mid-1980s were largely offset
by a substantial fall in the number of passengers,
making each journey actually more expensive to
the taxpayer. The number of buses did increase on
the already well-served routes, but fell by 11 per
cent in areas where the commercial return was
unattractive. Bus fares increased in real terms in
all parts of Great Britain after the mid-1980s.
Investment in the industry declined significantly
and, as a result, the average age of the buses on the
road rose by 30 per cent. The number of jobs in the
industry declined, and the real wages of bus
drivers declined relative to other manual workers.
Even the promise of competition was not really
fulfilled, as smaller operators sold out to big
conglomerates and ownership was gradually
concentrated in the hands of just three companies.[5]

THE IRISH EXPERIENCE: EIRCOM

In July 1999 the Minister for Public Enterprise, Ms
O'Rourke, told the Seanad that she was working
on a book about the privatisation of Telecom

Éireann (subsequently re-named Eircom). "Despite
the fact that the Taoiseach said we must not write
books about our time in Government, I intend to
write a book about Telecom. I am writing about
Telecom at the moment while the subject is fresh in
my mind." It is doubtful that the book was ever
written but if it was, it was never published. The
reason is obvious enough: it would be a sorry tale.

In May 1999, Mary O'Rourke addressed the
annual conference of the Communication Workers'
Union. Inevitably, given the nature of the audience,
the main subject of her speech was the forthcoming
privatisation of Telecom Éireann. She set out a very
clear vision of the overall policy objective of the
Initial Public Offering (IPO) or flotation.

> One of the objectives of the IPO that I mentioned
> earlier is that it should promote wider share
> ownership. It is my firm intention that there should
> be a significant tranche of the shares available to
> the citizens. This is a personal objective of mine and
> one I know that my Government colleagues share.
> It is entirely appropriate that the public reap the
> benefits of this success, the main benefit being the
> opportunity to be part of the future of the com-
> pany. Through a widespread shareholding the
> citizens, in conjunction with the employees, will be
> able to share in the successes of the company and to
> have a say in its development over the coming
> years ... This in my view is the essence of what
> being a public company means: a company which
> is literally owned by the people through the widest
> possible share ownership.

The message from the Oireachtas debates
which preceded privatisation was the same: this

AFTER THE BALL

would not be a case of fat cats getting their grubby paws on public assets. It could hardly be clearer. The Government's aim was to create a telecoms company that would be "literally owned by the people" who would "have a say in its development over the coming years". There would be no carving up of State assets. There would be no fat cats. ("I have no time for fat cats," Mary O'Rourke assured the public.)

If that really was the aim, the privatisation of Eircom was a complete failure. In less than two years, it had become completely clear that not only would the people not own a State-wide telecoms company, but that there would be no such company at all. Eircom was broken up. Its most profitable assets were knocked down cheaply to a global multinational, Vodafone. The rest was sold off for scrap. The fat cats got the cream and the putative shareholding democracy got the bum's rush.

Two and a quarter years after more than 500,000 investors ploughed their money into Eircom, the shares of the former State telecoms company were finally delisted from the Irish Stock Exchange in December 2001.

Some 50,000 investors, who bought and sold their shares within a matter of weeks of the flotation, made money. The remaining 450,000 shareholders, who held their shares, were left nursing a 30 per cent loss on the €3.90 (£3.07) they paid for each Eircom share. Ordinary shareholders were forced to sell out, whether they liked it or not, to the Valentia Telecommunications consortium.

They received €1.33 per share from Valentia as well as a $0.035 dividend. They were also left with declining Vodafone shares received when the British mobile phone group bought Eircom's subsidiary Eircell in an all-share deal.

The small investors' experience of the Eircom débâcle is likely to mean that any future State privatisation – even of the few State companies that could be floated on the market – will not involve small investors.

As an exercise in developing a culture of investment in stocks, the investors' involvement with Eircom was a disaster. For every short-term investor who made a quick profit when the shares initially spiked up to €4.50–€5.00, there were nine others who believed the hype about investing in a key element of national infrastructure and having a say in the long-term future of a public company and ended up with heavy losses and a painful lesson in powerlessness.

The essential result of the privatisation process is that Ireland ended up with no Irish-owned telecommunications company. Its land-line system is owned by Valentia, which comprises the US investment bank Goldman Sachs; Providence Equity Partners, a US private equity firm; Soros Private Equity Partners, affiliated to Soros Fund Management and part of the Hungarian-born financier Mr George Soros's empire; and Warburg Pincus, a private equity investment company. Sir Anthony O'Reilly, chairman of Independent News & Media, former chairman of HJ Heinz and a UK citizen, was the figurehead for the consortium but held an undisclosed stake in the business. The Eircom Employee Share Ownership Trust, controlled by Eircom's main unions – the Communication Workers Union and Impact – has 25 per cent of the equity and is the only substantial Irish owner of the Irish national phone system. Mobile telephony, a crucial and growing part of the communications infrastructure, is now controlled in the Republic by two British-based international groups – Vodafone and British Telecom.

THE IRISH EXPERIENCE: MEDICAL INSURANCE

The introduction of competition and the preparation for privatisation of the State medical insurance company VHI should have led, according to neo-liberal orthodoxy, to a lowering of health insurance premiums. In fact, they have had the opposite effect. In 2003, the VHI looked for an increase in premiums from its members of 8.5 per cent, on top of a rise of 18 per cent in 2002. When this increase is in effect, VHI charges will have increased by almost 50 per cent in two and a half years. Which raises a pretty fundamental question: if competition reduces prices to the consumer, how come medical insurance in Ireland keeps getting more expensive? Even allowing for the high rate of medical inflation, health insurance costs have risen dramatically.

The extra rise has two sources. One is the arrival of the British-based BUPA as a competitor for the VHI. BUPA has not been particularly successful. Its market share is around 10 per cent, and remarkably few of its customers seem to have switched from the VHI. But it has targeted younger people, mainly through group schemes in high-tech companies. These are the people who pay now for services they are most likely to need in thirty years' time. By taking them out of the VHI, and leaving the State-owned body with the older sections of the population, the arrival of BUPA has pushed up premium costs for the other 90 per cent of the insured population.

The other factor is that the VHI has been on the road to privatisation since 1999, when the Government decided to make it a commercial company. To make the VHI an attractive proposition for potential buyers it has to have significant cash reserves. Slowly, and with very little fuss, the VHI has been salting more and more money away. In the last five years, the VHI's reserves have almost doubled to €182 million. In 2002, it put away €14.7 million. In 2001, the figure was €28.2 million.

To be a solvent insurance company, the VHI should be taking in a little more in premiums than it is paying out in claims and salaries. For a public body with no need to generate profits for shareholders, this is all it needs to do. It did it for decades with no great problem, with the exception of the period in 1987 and 1988 when huge health cuts created a sudden rise in demand on the private hospital system. There is no reason why it could not continue to do so in the future.

A private commercial company, however, needs large reserves of cash. The VHI reckons that, as a commercial outfit, it will need reserves equivalent to 40 per cent of its income from premiums. So whereas in 1997, before the privatisation plan, the VHI's reserves were 20 per cent of its premium income, by 2002 they were 31 per cent. Where does the money for these reserves come from? The pocket of the subscriber, of course.

There is no reason to think that premiums will be cheaper if and when the VHI is sold off to the private sector. On the contrary, the buyers who will shell out around €300 million will want to make their money back fairly quickly and to return healthy profits thereafter. Given that they're hardly likely to get hospital consultants to charge a private company less than they charge the State, the only way to make those profits is to push premiums up even faster.

Also, why should BUPA have to compensate the VHI for leaving it with the older, more expensive members (the so-called "risk equalisation" policy) if the VHI is just another private commercial business? BUPA would have a very strong case for saying that such a policy is an improper interference in the competition between two private, profit-driven companies. Yet without risk equalisation, VHI premiums will rise even faster.

These experiences, and the abysmal record of the privatisation of public utilities elsewhere, ought to remind us that the urge to sell off State assets is motivated at least as much by the greed of élites and the ideological demands of neo-liberalism as by any rational economic analysis. At the very least, the case for the privatisation of any State company should be based on a real analysis of the international experience, a clear set of public policy goals and a fair-minded assessment of what public companies can and cannot achieve. For a small, extraordinarily open economy, the need to retain some level of national control is another reason for caution. In an economy where the State can influence so little, does it make sense to diminish State power even further by handing the public sector over to what will inevitably be transnational consortia whose only interest in Ireland would be profit?

8

THE VIEW FROM BOND STREET

If you walk down Bond Street in London's West End, you will see the best that the global marketplace has to offer. Chanel, Donna Karan, Tiffany, Ralph Lauren, Cartier, Bulgari, Dolce and Gabbana, Hermes, Bally: the magical brand names of global capitalism, the labels that add allure to the consumer and noughts to the bill. In the 1950s and 1960s, the Irish would most likely be found digging in the sewers beneath the street. Now they own much of it. The Bulgari shop went for UK£7 million and the Chanel emporium for UK£6.35 million in November 2002 – both to the same Irish investor, Aiden Brook. The Bally and Gerald Darel buildings are Irish owned, as is the Donna Karan store.

An unnamed Irish investor paid €36.75 million for the Prada building at 17–18 Old Bond Street in early 2003. Another Irish investor has splashed out UK£33 million for the Mulberry unit at 41–42 New Bond Street.[1] In all, spending on the street by Irish investors has amounted to over €230 million in less than three years. "It used to be Arabs, UK institutions, property companies, and Italian families who owned the street," declared the *Observer* just before Christmas 2002.

> Not any more. These days it's the Irish who rule Bond Street. Most of them operate in private syndicates who target trophy buildings. But there are a few heavy hitters led by Aiden Brook, Derek Quinlan and John McCormick who have spent tens of millions of pounds on properties.[2]

Irish individuals and institutions are now the second largest overseas buyers in the UK property market, trailing closely behind US investors.[3] Well-heeled Irish individuals, financial institutions and groupings of private investors jointly shelled out an estimated €1 billion on UK property in 2002. Irish funds such as DTZ Sherry FitzGerald and BCP Asset Management in association with Irish Life are major players in the London market.

According to *Business Plus* magazine in January 2003:

> How these funds work is that they leverage borrowings off the equity invested, enabling investors to scale up their investment. And banks like Anglo Irish have been lending big time to these fund investors, contenting themselves with taking just interest payments for now. Such schemes are also very attractive for the self-employed and shareholder directors who have self-administered pension funds. Using this mechanism, investors can get 42% relief on, say, paying €100,000 into their pension fund and then use the cash to redeem the borrowings incurred on the property invest-

ment. The minimum investment in DTZ Sherry's fund is €15,000 and it raised €10m in its first UK commercial property fund last August.

The huge scale of Irish investment in the UK property market tells us two things. One is that a great deal of wealth is being generated in Ireland. The other is that much of it goes abroad in unproductive investments that are facilitated and encouraged by the Irish tax system. And this in turn raises the key question for Ireland's efforts to sustain the prosperity of the 1990s. The great success of the Irish economy is its ability to attract foreign direct investment (FDI). In terms of stocks of inward FDI, Ireland ranked in eighth position among the fifteen members of the EU with FDI valued at €74.8 billion in 2001. This amounts to 2.8 per cent of the total in the EU and, in per capita terms, is the second highest after Belgium/Luxembourg.

The great weakness in the Irish economy, though, is the under-performance of Irish firms. The contrast between foreign-owned enterprises (FOEs) and indigenously owned enterprises (IOEs) in export terms is stark. FOEs sold almost 90 per cent of their output abroad, while IOEs' exports as a share of sales in 2001 stood at 38 per cent. As FOEs' export growth has consistently outstripped that of IOEs', the dominance of foreign firms in Irish merchandise exports grew, reaching 89 per cent of total exports.[4] FOEs are mostly large and capital intensive, enjoying considerable economies of scale. IOEs tend to be smaller in size and more labour intensive.

In terms of total manufacturing output as

measured by sales, FOEs (at €55.3 billion) out-performed IOEs (€16.7 billion) by a factor of 3.3.

The great difference between the foreign and indigenously owned sectors is that the level of gross value added per employee is more than five times greater in the former than the latter. In 2001 gross value added per employee in Irish-owned firms stood at €44,700, an increase in nominal terms of 10.7 per cent. Despite this strong growth, the gap widened, as value added per employee in foreign firms increased by 12.3 per cent to €226,000 per employee.

This huge difference is accounted for mostly by the foreign-owned firms being high-tech and employing highly skilled labour, while the Irish firms remain relatively low-tech. The food, drink and tobacco industries accounted for more than half of total sales by Irish-owned enterprises. In contrast, electronics, chemicals and computer-related industries accounted for three-quarters of FOE output.

The Irish- and foreign-owned companies don't even export to the same markets. The UK absorbed 51.3 per cent of IOE exports in 2001. While the EU has traditionally been the most important market for FOEs, "rest of the world" markets – mostly the US – grew to account for 41.8 per cent of the total in 2001.

The indigenous sector of the Irish economy is still dangerously dependent on the export of bulk commodity food (mostly beef and milk in a raw, unbranded, low-value added form) and live animals, which account for almost half of total indigenous exports but under 6 per cent of the total. These exports actually decreased slightly in 2001, to €5.8 billion, and grew in the first half of 2002 by just 1 per cent.

The cost of this imbalance is high, and it points to the underlying weaknesses in the Irish economy. In 2001, Ireland, in spite of its huge trade surplus, ran a deficit of €17.4 billion on its trade in services, reflecting payment of inter-affiliate management fees and royalties charged by foreign corporations to their Irish subsidiaries for head office services, such as finance, administration and marketing services and the use of manufacturing technologies developed abroad. Total payments abroad for royalties and licences (R&L) were just under €10 billion in 2001. It is highly likely, however, that these payments are substantially under-reported given the preference of multinational corporations to declare profits in Ireland to take advantage of the lower corporate tax rates here.

Also flowing out of the Irish economy, however, is the very large and increasing amount of Irish investment overseas. While investment in Irish-owned firms at home remains inadequate, and the companies therefore remain under-developed, the stock of foreign assets in the hands of Irish firms rose to US$23.9 billion in 2001, an increase of 30 per cent on 2000 and a tenfold increase on 1990. Investment outflows from Ireland grew by 30 per cent to reach €6.6 billion in 2001.

Ireland, for example, is now the ninth largest source of foreign direct investment in the US. The total of Irish investment in the US reached $18.5

billion (€16 billion) in 2001, the latest year for which statistics are available. This represents an explosion in Irish business expansion into the US in the last decade. It is more than double the value of Irish investment in the US in 1998 ($8.4 billion) and almost four times the total in 1996 ($4.8 billion).

Ten years previously, in 1991, it amounted to barely $2 billion.[5] Elan, for instance, made one of the 50 biggest acquisitions in the US in 2000 when it took over Dura Pharmaceuticals for $1.7 billion.

Much of this investment is productive and may help to strengthen Irish firms in the long term. But the huge inflows and outflows of capital cannot disguise that Irish-owned businesses are relatively poor contributors to the economy. There is a sense in which the Irish economy became global before it became national. The staple of many national economies – small and medium-sized indigenous businesses – is a muted presence in Ireland.

This has nothing to do with the old stereotype of the Irish not being natural entrepreneurs or of Ireland having an anti-enterprise culture. The Global Entrepreneurship Monitor (GEM) 2001 study found that 7.2 per cent of the Irish population were trying to start a new business. This indicates that:

- over 160,000 adults are currently engaged in the process of starting a business
- approximately 110,000 adults currently partly or fully own and operate a business started since 1998

- almost 5,000 adults believe that the new venture, which they are currently planning, will employ more than 50 people after five years

According to the VAT registration figures compiled by the European Small and Medium Enterprise (SME) Observatory, Ireland had one of the highest rates of new business start-ups in the EU during the period 1995–2000.[6] According to the Flash Eurobarometer survey on entrepreneurship, Ireland has one of the higher propensities towards self-employment in Europe. The EU average is 51 per cent whereas 61 per cent of Irish people have a propensity for self-employment, with the US at approximately 70 per cent for the same measure.

The problem is that Irish SMEs are not very good at creating jobs. The proportion of total employment accounted for by such businesses is lower in Ireland than the EU average. Ninety-nine per cent of Irish companies are SMEs, but they account for only 51 per cent of total employment. In the rest of Europe, SMEs make up roughly the same proportion of all companies, but account for 66 per cent of employment. The contrast is particularly stark when it comes to small businesses, defined as those employing fewer than ten people. In the EU as a whole, this sector of the economy employs 33 per cent of the work-force. In Ireland it employs 18 per cent.

Ireland has had long experience of the reality that an open economy does not necessarily ensure that indigenous industry thrives. Indeed, the first

30 years of Ireland's integration into the world economy was itself a case in point. As the National Economic and Social Council puts it:

> The adjustment of indigenous enterprises to international competition failed more often than it succeeded. Job creation was insufficient, old jobs were lost at a remarkable rate and unemployment increased. High levels of savings and corporate profits were not matched by investment in the Irish economy.[7]

Having been there before, Irish people know that they could face this problem again, especially in the new climate of global economic downturn.

The Irish experience shows with striking clarity that success in the globalised marketplace is not at all incompatible with social squalor. Even at a simple level, the failure to invest in public services is costly. False economies end up draining resources from both the private and public sectors. To take just one example, the lack of a decent, well-financed public transport service in Dublin doesn't just hurt citizens trying to go about their lives with the least possible stress. It also costs money.

In August 2001, for example, the Small Firms Association published the results of a comparative study of the time taken for a simple business trip in various cities around the world. It tested the time taken for five kilograms of goods to travel five kilometres. In Singapore, the journey took 9 minutes. In London, the average journey time was 13 minutes. In Amsterdam, Paris and Helsinki, it took a quarter of an hour or less for the goods to reach their destination. In New York, it was 17.5 minutes. Bombay was bad: 37 minutes. In Dublin, however, it took an average of 57 minutes. The only city that was worse was Calcutta. In the morning rush hour in Dublin the average delivery time was 1 hour 20 minutes. According to the Small Firms Association, all of this "impacts on business by increasing travel-to-work times, exacerbating the bottlenecks in the movement of goods and eroding the competitive edge of business".

This in turn has huge costs for the public bus company, Bus Átha Cliath. Currently 802 trips operated by BÁC run over their schedule on a daily basis. This results in the company incurring unscheduled operating time of approximately 239 hours per day. The annual cost of congestion to the company rose from €34.87 million in 2001 to €49.37 million in 2003 – a 42 per cent increase over the period.[8] In 2002/2003 BÁC trips are scheduled to achieve an average speed of 13.6 k.p.h. at peak time and 15.8 k.p.h. during the off peak. This compares with a peak speed of 14.6 k.p.h. and an off peak speed of 17.3 k.p.h. in 2001. If BÁC could operate at average international speeds, it could run its current schedule in approximately 3,313 fewer hours per day, saving at current rates almost €50 million a year.

Intelligent public investment and a long-term commitment to having efficient and attractive public transport run for the benefit of citizens would save vast sums for both private business and the taxpayer. But this kind of investment is

labelled as subsidy and thus rendered ideolog-
ically *ultra vires*.

What all of this points to is that, in the long-
term, globalisation, even for its star performer
Ireland, is not enough. Attracting large-scale
foreign direct investment gave Ireland a sudden,
extraordinary boom. But keeping Ireland prosperous in the long term means doing much more
than simply keeping Corporation Tax rates low
and being nice to multinational corporations. It
means creating an economy in which Irish-owned
enterprises can generate as much wealth and
employment as the foreign-owned sector. That
requires a huge increase in creativity, innovation
and quality.

And that means creating a society in which
large sections of the population are not consigned
to poverty, illiteracy and ill health, in which the
taxation system doesn't actively encourage people
with money to salt it away in tax avoidance
schemes and in which the values that lay behind
the boom – social solidarity, the inclusion of
women, public investment in education, the
communal and collective ethic of the Internet – are
rediscovered.

If the Irish boom is misunderstood as the
product of neo-conservative economics, the
agenda for sustaining prosperity is obvious: more
tax cuts, more privatisation, a weaker State, an
expansion of the ethos in which Irish people are to
be understood as consumers rather than as
citizens. If the boom is understood for what it was
– a complex product of left-of-centre values which

has not ended the spectacle of social squalor even while removing the excuse for it – the agenda is equally clear. Without a strong, active, imaginative public sphere in which all citizens have the capacity to participate, we will look back on the boom years as a time of unfulfilled promises.

APPENDIX

Table A.1 Waiting lists for public patients by hospital, mid-2003

Hospital	Waiting
Beaumount Hospital	4240
Cavan General	609
Coombe Women's Hospital	43
Cork University Hospital	806
Ennis General	0
Holles St	0
James Connolly Memorial	706
Kilcreene Orthopaedic	144
Letterkenny General	2563
Limerick Regional	1137
Longford/Westmeath Hospital	51
Louth County Hospital	0
Mater Hospital	3918

APPENDIX

Hospital	Waiting
Mayo General	75
Mercy Hospital, Cork	259
Merlin Park Regional, Galway	330
Monaghan General	1
Naas General	0
National Rehabilitation Hospital	135
Nenagh General	0
Our Lady of Lourdes, NEHB	281
Our Lady's Hospital, Crumlin	1029
Our Lady's Hospital, Navan	604
Portiuncula, Ballinasloe	4
Portlaoise General	30
Regional Orthopaedic, Croom	70
Roscommon General	2
Rotunda Hospital	0
Royal Eye and Ear, Dublin	976
Sligo Regional Hospital	782
St Infirmary/Royal Vic, Cork	177
St Vincents, Elm Park	3302
Tallaght Hospital	1442
Temple St, Children's	751
Tralee General	171
Tullamore General	548
University CH, Galway	950
Waterford Regional	1338
Wexford General	32

Source: irishhealth.com, Waiting List Watch

Table A.2 Situation of women on State boards and bodies of public interest: October 2003

State board	Men	Women	% Women
Aer Lingus	11	1	8
Aer Rianta	8	1	11
Arts Council	9	8	47
Board of the Court Service	11	6	35
Bord Bia	12	3	20
Bord na gCon/Irish Greyhound Board	7	0	0
Bord Fáilte Éireann	6	2	25
Bord Gais Éireann	7	1	12
Bord Iascaigh Mhara	5	1	17
An Bord Pinsean/Pensions Board	10	7	41
An Bord Pleanála	7	5	42
Bord Scannán na hÉireann/Irish Film Board	4	3	43
Bus Átha Cliath/Dublin Bus	8	1	11
Central Bank of Ireland	12	0	0
CERT	10	8	44

State board	Men	Women	% Women
An Chomhairle Oidhreachta/The Heritage Council	9	5	36
Coillte Teoranta/The Irish Forestry Board	8	1	11
Combat Poverty Agency	3	10	77
Coras Iompair Éireann (CIE)	8	3	37
Dublin Transportation Office	14	1	7
Electricity Supply Board	10	2	17
Enterprise Ireland	6	5	36
Equality Authority	5	8	61
FÁS	12	5	29
Food Safety Authority of Ireland	8	2	20
Forfás	9	3	25
Health and Safety Authority	8	3	27
Higher Education Authority	10	6	37
Iarnród Éireann/Irish Rail	6	2	25
IDA Ireland	10	2	17
Irish Aid Advisory Committee	7	3	30
Irish Blood Transfusion Service	5	5	50

State board	Men	Women	% Women
Irish Sports Council	7	3	30
Legal Aid Board	4	7	64
The Medical Council	23	6	21
National Council for Curriculum and Assessment	26	5	17
National Disability Authority	11	9	45
National Economic and Social Council	26	5	16
National Lottery	7	1	12
National Roads Authority	9	5	36
National Theatre Society	5	4	44
National Treasury Management Company	7	0	0
An Post	11	3	21
RTÉ	4	4	50
Teagasc	9	2	18
Údarás na Gaeltachta	18	2	10
Working Group on Court Jurisdiction	16	2	11

Source: *Irish Politics: Jobs for the Boys*, National Women's Council of Ireland

NOTES

1. GLOBAL IRELAND

[1] Orlando Figes, *A People's Tragedy: A History of the Russian Revolution*, London, 1996, pp. 72–3

[2] See the *World Development Report 2003* of the World Bank

[3] See *State of the World 1999*, Wordwatch Institute, New York, 1999, pp. 7–10

[4] See Kieran A. Kennedy, "The Context of Economic Development", in Goldthorpe and Whelan (eds) *The Development of Industrial Society in Ireland*, Oxford, 1992, p. 7

[5] J. J. Lee, *Ireland 1912–1985: Politics and Society*, Cambridge, 1989, pp. 514–5

[6] Fred McMahon, *Road to Growth: How Lagging Economies Become Prosperous*, Atlantic Institute for Market Studies, Halifax, Nova Scotia, 2000, Chapter 2 "The Celtic Tiger"

[7] D. A. Coleman, "Demography and Migration in Ireland, North and South", in Heath, Breen and

Whelan (eds) *Ireland North and South*, Oxford, 1999, p. 86
[8] Garret FitzGerald, *The Irish Times*, November 11th 2000

2. COPYRIGHT AND COPYLEFT

[1] Quoted in John Naughton, *A Brief History of the Future*, Weidenfeld and Nicholson, London, 1999, p. 75
[2] Barry M. Leiner, et al., *A Brief History of the Internet*, http://www.isoc.org/internet/history/brief.shtml#Origins
[3] Quoted in Naughton, p. 196
[4] Ibid., p. 183
[5] Ibid., p. 230
[6] Ibid., p. 107
[7] Quoted in John Sulston and Georgina Ferry, *The Common Thread*, London, 2002, p. 161
[8] Ibid., p. 274
[9] Ibid., pp. 261, 279, 274

3. FISCAL RECTITUDE

[1] Desmond McCarthy, *Social Policy and Macroeconomics: The Irish Experience*, Working Paper No: 2736, December 2001
[2] See Comptroller and Auditor General, *Report of Investigation into the Administration of DIRT*, July 1999
[3] *Report of the Inspectors Appointed to Inquire into the Affairs of Ansbacher (Cayman) Limited*, Vol. 1, 2002, p. 458
[4] Maev-Ann Wren, *Unhealthy State*, New Island, Dublin, 2002, pp. 88–89

4. POVERTY AND INEQUALITY

[1] CORI Justice Commission, *Achieving Inclusion*, Dublin, 2003

[2] Eurostat, Statistics in focus, Population and social conditions, no. 3/2003, *Social Protection in Europe*

[3] Eurostat, *Social Protection*, Brussels, 2003

[4] Vincentian Partnership for Social Justice, *One Long Struggle*, Dublin, 2001

[5] Profile of Households Accommodated by Dublin City Council, 2001

[6] Department of Social and Family Affairs, statistical bulletin 2001

[7] *Achieving Inclusion*, 2003

[8] *The Irish Times*, October 29th 1997

[9] Patrick Clancy and Joy Wall, *Social Background of Higher Education Entrants*, HEA, Dublin, 2000.

[10] These figures come from *The Health of Irish People*, Department of Health, Dublin, 2002, and Joe Barry et al., *Inequalities in Health in Ireland: Hard Facts*, TCD School of Community Medicine, Dublin, 2001

[11] *Equity of Access to Hospital Care*, National Economic and Social Forum, Dublin, 2001

5. ON THE OUTSIDE

[1] This figure and those that follow are from *Early School Leavers: Forum Report 24*, NESF, Dublin, 2002

[2] Statement by John Carr, INTO General Secretary, on Educational Disadvantage, September 24th 2002

[3] *The Irish Times*, June 16th 2003

[4] Polly Toynbee, *Guardian Education*, June 3rd 2003

[5] See *Irish Politics: Jobs for the Boys*, National Women's Council of Ireland, Dublin, November 2002

[6] *The Irish Times*, March 13th 2003

[7] Unless stated otherwise, these figures are from the database of the Gender Equality Unit of the Department of Justice, Equality and Law Reform

[8] *The Irish Times*, September 9th 1999

[9] Barrett and Callan (eds), *How Unequal?*, ESRI/ Oaktree Press, Dublin, 2000

[10] Department of the Environment and Local Government Annual Report of the National Traveller Accommodation Consultative Committee, 2001.

[11] See *The Irish Times*, July 11th 2003

[12] *Beyond the Pale: Asylum-seeking Children and Social Exclusion in Ireland*, Irish Refugee Council, Dublin, 2001

6. WHY ONLY THE LITTLE PEOPLE PAY TAXES

[1] Des Crowley, *Sunday Business Post*, October 7th 2001

[2] All of these cases are real and are taken from the Report of the Comptroller and Auditor General for 2001.

[3] Mary Coughlan TD, Minister for Social and Family Affairs, Press Release, April 6th 2003

[4] Effective Tax Rates for High Earning Individuals, Budget 2003

[5] The 2002 figure was given by the Minister for Finance in a written reply to questions from Richard Bruton TD. See *The Sunday Tribune*, July 6th 2003

7. SELLING OFF THE FAMILY SILVER

[1] Steve Thomas, "The Impact of Privatisation on Electricity Prices in Britain", presentation to the IDEC National Seminar on Public Utilities, Sao Paulo, August 6th–8th, 2002

[2] Jerrold Oppenheim, *US Electric Utilities*, Brussels, 2001

[3] House of Commons Select Committee on the Environment, *Seventh Report 1999-2000: Water Prices and the Environment HC 597*, London, November 14th 2000

[4] Emanuele Lobina, "UK Water Privatisation: A Briefing", University of Greenwich, February 2001

[5] David Bayliss, *Buses in Great Britain: Privatisation, Deregulation and Competition*, World Bank, 1999

8. THE VIEW FROM BOND STREET

[1] *Sunday Business Post*, June 8th 2003

[2] Nick Mathiason, *Observer*, December 22nd 2002

[3] *Business Plus*, January 2003

[4] These figures and those that follow are taken from *International Trade & Investment Report 2002*, Forfás, Dublin, June 2003

[5] *The Irish Times*, May 19th 2003

[6] "Entrepreneurship in Ireland: A Paper Prepared for the National Competitiveness Council", Goodbody Economic Consultants, Dublin, November 2002

[7] NESC, *An Investment in Quality: Services, Inclusion and Enterprise*, Dublin, 2002

[8] Bus Átha Cliath, *Cost of Congestion Report*, Dublin, June 2003

SUPPORT TASC – A THINK TANK FOR ACTION ON SOCIAL CHANGE

"The limited development of think tanks is a striking feature [of Ireland] for such bodies could do much to focus new thinking about the country's future democratic and political development"

(Report to the Joseph Rowntree Charitable Trust, 2002)

Ireland, almost uniquely in Europe, has relatively few think tanks of any kind and, prior to the establishment of **tasc**, none whose sole agenda is to foster new thinking on ways to create a more progressive and equal society. Such an independent public policy think tank is long overdue and urgently needed in Ireland.

Your support is essential – to do its work **tasc** must keep a distance from political and monetary pressure in order to protect the independence of its agenda. If you would like to make a contribution to **tasc** – a think tank for action on social change, please send your donation to the address below.

With many thanks,
Fintan O'Toole

Donations to:
tasc
A think tank for action on social change
25 South Frederick St
Dublin 2
Phone: 00 353 1 6169050
E-mail: contact@tascnet.ie
www.tascnet.ie